# Washingtoniana

# HANK HARRISON
# HARRISON
## FOR
# PRESIDENT

# Also by Fred J. Eckert

*FIJI: Some Enchanted Islands*

*FIJI: Pacific Paradise*

*FIJI: The Way The World Should Be*

*ROME: The Eternal City*

*TONGA: The Friendly Islands*

# HANK
# HARRISON
### FOR
# PRESIDENT

### A Novel By

## Fred J. Eckert

VANDAMERE PRESS
a division of AB Associates

Published by:
Vandamere Press
A division of AB Associates
P.O. Box 5243
Arlington, Virginia 22205


Copyright © 1992 Fred J. Eckert


ISBN 0-918339-24-3


Library of Congress Cataloging-in-Publication Data

Eckert, Fred J., 1941-
    Hank Harrison for president / Fred J. Eckert
      p.    cm.
    ISBN 0-918339-24-3
    I. Title
  PS3555.C56H3   1991
813'.54—dc20                                              91-37664
                                                             CIP

Manufactured in the United States of America. This book is set in
Palatino by Scott Photographics.

To my wife, Karen,
and to our children,
Douglas, Brian and Cynthia

## Author's Note

This book is a work of fiction. That means the story isn't true. I made it up. The whole thing. Names, characters, places and incidents are either the product of my imagination or are used fictitiously. Any resemblance to actual events or locales or to persons, living or dead, is entirely coincidental. Coincidentally enough, the names of some of the characters in this novel happen to be the same as the names of some dear friends of mine. For the most part, my friends bear little or no resemblance to the characters who share their names, except for the fact that my friends are also characters. Most of these friends do resemble living persons—although a couple of them sometimes act more like dead people. I used their names because it saved me the bother of having to make up quite so many fictitious names. Besides, it was sort of fun for me to do that, and they get a kick out of it, too. Hank Harrison, by the way, wasn't a friend of mine until I made him up.

# One

It was probably inevitable. Sooner or later it was bound to happen. Someone with the unbelievably unbefitting credentials of a Hank Harrison would become President of the United States.

And the public would accept it.

Hell, they'd actually like it.

But no one ever imagined it would happen quite this soon. No one ever dreamed it would happen quite this way.

Through a bizarre set of circumstances, 57-year-old Hank Harrison of Freka, Arkansas, was sitting in the White House as President of the United States.

The bizarre set of circumstances did not include an election.

And now Hank Harrison was running for President as the incumbent.

Only a few months earlier he had been best known as the owner of the only dry-cleaning store in a little town in Arkansas. Yet in this very short time he had become not only President, but a very popular, almost beloved, President.

Already most people were calling him "another Reagan." Older people were calling him "another Ike."

And everybody—everybody—agreed that come the first Tuesday after the first Monday in November, Hank Harrison of Freka, Arkansas, would be elected President of the United States in his own right.

Hank had ended up in the nation's highest office, the most powerful post in the world, without having been elected to it.

That was a bit unusual, but far from unheard of. After all, it was true of more than one out of every five of our Presidents. Nine others had taken the oath of office as President without having been first elected to the office—Gerald Ford, Lyndon Johnson, Harry Truman, Calvin Coolidge, Teddy Roosevelt, Chester Arthur, Andrew Johnson, Millard Fillmore and John Tyler.

Hank Harrison had become President without ever having held any elective office.

That, too, was unusual, although certainly not unheard of. A half dozen others had become President without ever having held elective office—Dwight Eisenhower, Herbert Hoover, William Howard Taft, Ulysses S. Grant, Zachary Taylor and William Henry Harrison.

And, of course, as everyone knows, here in the land of "majority rule" democracy, more than one-third of our Presidents won the White House while receiving less than half of the votes cast in the Presidential election.

More people voted against than for Abraham Lincoln and John Kennedy and Richard Nixon and Harry Truman and John Quincy Adams and James Polk and Zachary Taylor and James Buchanan and Rutherford Hayes and James Garfield and Benjamin Harrison and Grover Cleveland and Woodrow Wilson—and they all still became President.

In fact, Cleveland and Wilson share the distinction of having more people vote against them than for them two times—and, of course, each still became President both times.

Poor Samuel J. Tilden had more people vote for him than against him—only to watch Rutherford B. Hayes be sworn in as President. But Hayes pulled one more vote than Tilden in the Electoral College thanks to some sneaky manipulations by the carpetbaggers which threw three Southern states to Hayes. That caused such an uproar that Congress created a special election commission to validate the returns, which, as everyone knows, only perpetuated the controversy because that congressional commission split along party lines and also awarded Tilden's prize to Hayes by one vote.

Perhaps Tilden didn't think it was all that unusual. After all, fifty-two years earlier John Quincy Adams had lost both the popular vote and the electoral vote to Andrew Jackson the first time they ran against one another. Yet it was Adams who took the oath of office as President in 1825, because no one had received a majority in the Electoral College and the House of Representatives picked Adams even though Jackson had received 15 more votes than Adams in the electoral vote and 44,804 more of the popular votes.

Of course George Washington ran unopposed both times and James Monroe's "Era of Good Feelings" was such a hit that when he ran for re-election there was only one vote cast against him in the Electoral College.

Legend has it that the only reason that lone elector, a man from New Hampshire named William Plumer, voted against Monroe was that Plumer felt strongly that George Washington should remain the only American ever to be elected President by a unanimous vote, which, of course, was then and remains a good idea. The truth is that Plumer was pledged to Monroe and broke his pledge because he decided Monroe was too big a spender.

There are a lot of interesting facts about our Presidents and how they got there and stayed there. But historians are going to have to say that the way Hank Harrison became President of the United States was truly the most unusual.

What was not only unusual but also unheard of in the case of Hank Harrison was that, in addition to assuming the Presidency without having been elected to the office and without even having held any elective office, he had also taken up work in the Oval Office without ever having held any important position in government or in the military.

Or, for that matter, even any unimportant position in those fields.

Without ever having served as a corporate executive or a college president.

Or anything that anybody anywhere could seriously claim as even remotely approaching preparation for the presidency.

He was the ultimate outsider.

Up until the time he was catapulted into the Presidency, Hank Harrison wasn't known to more than a handful of people outside Freka, Arkansas, and most of them were either relatives or friends who had moved away. It should be noted, however, that just about everyone in Freka did know him and just about all of them did like him.

Probably the strangest component of the whole strange saga was the particularly peculiar performance of the Supreme Court of the United States.

And yet the public apparently felt comfortable enough with this astonishing turn of events.

Or indifferent enough.

Or whatever.

Voters clearly seemed to be of a mind to voluntarily entrust the leadership of the nation into the hands of this dry-cleaner from Arkansas. All the polls showed that.

It was all simply one of those great American success stories the public loves so much. At least so went the conventional wisdom.

There were some who considered the events they had witnessed to be the ultimate triumph of public relations symbols over public policy substance—proof positive that the American public is less interested in sound government than in superb gimmickry. But they were clearly a small minority. The news media did their job and saw to it that this point of view was adequately and appropriately covered. But few noticed. And fewer cared.

People seemed to enjoy the show.

And no one enjoyed it more than Bill Schulz.

It had been Bill Schulz's idea. The whole thing. All a product of his remarkably creative imagination.

And his weird sense of humor.

The news media was calling Bill Schulz the ultimate political consultant. They were right about that.

They were also saying that, being about to succeed in electing his second President, he had achieved everything a political consultant could dream of. They were wrong about that.

For Bill Schulz's dream was larger than their imaginations.

He had indeed seen one dream come true and it was obvious to just about everyone that in a few weeks he would see a second dream come true.

But he had another dream—a really big dream. But it was still only a dream.

Bill Schulz had known for a long time now exactly what it was that he most wanted.

He wanted to be the one who would do what all the truly great political consultants secretly dream of doing but none had dared attempt.

# *Two*

More than any other person, more than any combination of other persons, Bill Schulz had been responsible for setting in motion the chain of events which had first turned an obscure Governor of New Hampshire named John William Newell into President of the United States and then put a totally unknown dry-cleaning store owner from Arkansas named Hank Harrison into the Oval Office.

It had all started with one simple far-out idea.

One simple far-out idea which, it turned out, made sense. And history.

One simple far-out idea which, apparently, no one else in the entire history of American politics had ever thought of.

Jack Newell was the 51-year-old Governor of New Hampshire and Bill Schulz was a 38-year-old vice president of the Washington-based advertising and public relations agency which handled the state's tourism account when the two men first met.

Because tourism is so important to the economy of little New Hampshire, the Governor was personally and deeply involved in just about anything that touched upon it and thus he and Schulz came to work closely together. They worked together so well that they soon became fast friends at work and then outside work as well.

People said they were an odd couple. It was often noted that each looked and acted the role that the other had.

Bill Schulz looked like a Hollywood casting director's idea of a governor. He was tall, just over six feet one inch, thin, handsome, clear blue eyes, with a full head of wavy gray hair. He wore only tailor-made suits of the finest quality and his tie was almost always Gucci, Fendi, Valentino or Armani. His shoes were always Ferragamo.

Bill had attended the College of William and Mary, where he majored in business, and he also had a law degree from the University of Virginia, although he had never really practiced law because he found the business world, especially the advertising/public relations business, more fun. In public, and in the company of persons he did not yet know well enough, he acted the way he dressed—sophisticated, urbane, conservative, distinguished.

It was only in private with persons with whom he was very comfortable that Bill Schulz let loose his nuclear-powered imagination and weird sense of humor.

Governor Jack Newell, on the other hand, did not look like a Hollywood depiction of a governor. He was merely average looking and of average height, five-ten. He was a bit plump and he had thinning gray hair. He thought Gucci, Fendi, Ferragamo and Armani were the names of sports cars. He bought his suits and his ties and his shoes from whomever had them on sale when he needed some.

What he had most in common with Bill Schulz was that he, too, was a man of sharp intelligence. His degree, however, was in veterinary medicine from the University of New Hampshire.

In public with people whom he did not know at all Jack Newell was exactly as he was in private with people he knew very well—down-to-earth, no airs. The kind of man who reminded you of the stereotype nice-guy, next-door neighbor.

Bill Schulz, trained lawyer, successful businessman and advertising /public relations whiz, was fascinated by politics in general and political intrigue in particular. Jack Newell, veterinarian and accidental politician, wasn't.

One day, over coffee, Schulz matter-of-factly volunteered a political strategy idea as he listened to the Governor discuss with his secretary a problem he was having with the Legislature. He noticed later that the Governor acted on his suggestion.

In time he began making more and more suggestions. No one thought anything of it and no one particularly seemed to notice that it was happening, but in a very short time the advertising/public relations whiz from Washington had become the Governor's most trusted political advisor.

Probably the reason it happened was that, deep down, Jack Newell had little real interest in political matters. He was an excellent veterinarian and he was by nature a very good problem solver, but he had run for Governor mostly out of a sense of duty. A genuine rare case of someone's seeking office because he wanted to do something rather than because he wanted to be something.

His wife hated politics. His children were indifferent. And his closest friends were mostly fellow veterinarians who had, unfortunately for him but fortunately for them, moved to warmer climates.

So Bill Schulz had just sort of stumbled into a void. Jack Newell found him smart, honest, decent—and fun. His influence upon the Governor steadily increased.

Then came the idea. The big one. The one that made history.

At first they both just laughed about it. Chuckled about it each time Bill Schulz managed to work it into a conversation. Just another example of his weird sense of humor, wasn't it? The sort of thing that made Bill such fun to be around. What a funny idea! Boy, wouldn't something like *that* be funny!

The Governor was bored. And he told Schulz so. He had

done what he had set out to do as Governor and all this ceremonial malarkey he had to put up with in order to be in the position to do the serious work was, well, boring. Incredibly boring. And somewhat demeaning, too.

He told Schulz he wouldn't run again. He said the only thing that bothered him about that decision was that he really didn't know what he *did* want to do. He did not feel like going back to his veterinary practice. He said that his wife would be happy when he told her he wasn't going to run again, but she sure as hell would ask what he *did* plan to do. A man in his early fifties who says he doesn't know what he wants to do in life sounds like he's having a mid-life crisis and that would only make her worry and pester him with lots of questions.

Bored with being governor. Not wanting to return to his veterinary practice. Not financially independent enough to retire. And too young to retire even if he could afford to.

Bill Schulz saw his chance to really go for his great idea. "Who's going to win the New Hampshire primary?" he asked Jack Newell.

"Who cares?" the Governor replied.

"Exactly," said Schulz.

"What?" said the Governor.

"Nobody really cares which one of those two guys wins, right?" said Schulz.

"So what?" said Jack Newell. "One of them is going to be our next President."

"Only if you and I let that happen," said Schulz.

Bill Schulz reminded Governor Newell that all the polling data indicated that the two leading candidates in their party were running neck and neck.

That the voters didn't perceive any important differences between them.

That neither of them inspired any deep enthusiasm from more than a handful of the surprisingly few voters who presently indicated a preference for either one of them.

That the main reason most people gave for indicating a preference for one of them was that they wanted to vote against the other one.

Schulz asked the Governor what he thought all that meant and Jack Newell replied: "It means not many people really give a shit who's President."

What it also meant, Schulz argued, was that opportunity was knocking at their door and all they had to do was open it and they'd step right into the White House.

"Isn't it true that whoever wins the New Hampshire presidential primary immediately becomes just about the best-known person in the country?" Schulz asked. "Overnight one of the most talked about persons in the world, right? Overnight the front-runner for the Party's nomination, right? And this year that means automatically the front-runner for the Presidency, too, almost a certain winner, right?"

"So?" said the Governor.

"So enter the primary," said Schulz. "You'll win it. No problem. And then you'll be President."

Governor Newell rolled his eyes and shook his head. "You really are crazy, aren't you?"

"You can be a smart ass if that's the height of your ambition," Bill Schulz said to his friend Jack Newell with an intensity the Governor had not before heard in his voice or witnessed in his eyes. "But if you want to use that brain of yours for something useful, why don't you try to think of anything I've said so far that isn't right on the mark. Go ahead— anything!"

Schulz kept at it: "You're a very popular guy here. You won big. People like you. They respect you. In the polling data I've seen they attribute qualities to you that we could easily market as 'Presidential.' And, perhaps just as important, New Hampshire voters like doing something a bit different now and then."

And at it: "Enter the race and you'd pull a hell of a lot of the protest against each of the other two that is right there under the surface.

And at it: "Plus one hell of a lot of the voters who have no strong feelings about either one of them—and, remember, that's most of them—just might enjoy voting for someone they know. Especially if we can make them feel that the someone they know has the qualities they associate with the position."

"Ever wonder why no one else ever thought of it?" asked Governor Newell.

"Whoever is Governor of New Hampshire automatically has a crack at the Presidency," said Bill Schulz. "I don't know why none of them ever figured it out. It's so obvious. Hell, I figured that out when I was just a kid."

"And I suppose the reason no Governor of New Hampshire has ever gone on to become President is that we keep picking Governors who are too dumb to see something even a little kid could figure out?" said Jack Newell.

Schulz reminded the Governor that what he was saying was that any Governor of New Hampshire automatically has a crack at the Presidency—that is, a considerably better opportunity than others enjoy—simply because he is so much better positioned to seize the opportunity of the make-it-or-break-it New Hampshire primary than almost any other elected official in the nation.

The Governor remarked that running for President, or even talking about running for President, was pretty serious business.

Schulz argued that times were changing.

Maybe it was the intoxicating appeal of the excitement. Maybe it was the allure of doing something truly unique. Maybe it was the mesmerizing hope of becoming a character in the history books. Whatever. Governor Jack Newell of New Hampshire looked squarely into the eyes of his good friend Bill Schulz and uttered the words which Schulz would never forget as long as he lived.

Words that would determine who would occupy the highest office in the land, the most powerful position in the world.

Words that would change the course of history.

"Who gives a shit?" said Jack Newell. "Why not?"

Not quite up there with, "Give me liberty or give me death."

Not quite as eloquent as "Nothing to fear but fear itself" or "Ask not what your country can do for you; ask what you can do for your country."

Not quite another, "Read my lips."

Not eloquent words. Not even particularly memorable words. Just ordinary words.

But ordinary words which changed the course of history.

# Three

J ack Newell's campaign for the presidency was what the
politicos like to call a textbook case.

That is, he won.

Oh, a lot of people snickered when the Governor of New
Hampshire announced that he was entering the New Hampshire primary and running for President. But not for long.

The giggling stopped the day he won the primary.

Some tried to disparage his victory by pointing out that
he had the "home court" advantage. But that didn't matter
to Jack Newell. More important, it didn't matter to Bill Schulz.

What mattered to Bill Schulz was that the results proved
his theory. Jack Newell received such an incredible avalanche
of publicity that overnight he became one of the best-known
persons in the country. Just as Bill Schulz had said would
happen.

It was then just a matter of keeping a good thing going.

Looking back on it all, what people seem to remember
best is that the campaign sort of reminded them of the films
they had seen of John F. Kennedy's race for the White House.

Jack Newell sounded like John Kennedy. He couldn't help
that. The accent is a cross New Englanders bear. Also, his
campaign theme somehow reminded people of Kennedy.

That wasn't accidental. That was Schulz's doing. Jack Newell talked about getting America moving. Getting America moving forward. And doing it with vigor.

Generalities, sure. But glittering generalities. Good glittering generalities.

Less than a week following his New Hampshire primary victory, the Governor of New Hampshire, yesterday's unknown and today's man of destiny, was being hailed as a not-so-good-looking Kennedy.

That's what the nation's news media called him. And that's what people started thinking.

Few stopped to ponder that if one accepts the proposition that moving is somewhat better than standing still going nowhere—and most people seem to—then it is just a matter of deciding which direction to move in and most people do seem to favor the forward option. You can move backwards. You can move sideways. Or you can move forward. Standing for moving forward seemed a pretty safe bet. (At election time, it does not occur to anyone that it is also possible to move up or to move down—so that's not even worth mentioning.) As for the vigor bit, well, that certainly seemed safe, too. Sizzle usually sounds better than fizzle, especially at election time.

Some in the press did note that the campaign was not turning on the great issues of the day but rather on fleeting images.

A few columnists professed a longing for some sort of a rerun of the Nixon-Kennedy debate, just as they always do, although none of them noted, just as they never do, that in that great debate Nixon and Kennedy talked mostly about two tiny islands in the Formosa Strait which haven't been heard about since. Nor did any of the great commentators note that the talk of the country right after that great debate was that Nixon had forgotten to shave, a small but critical oversight which apparently made many 1960 voters judge him unqualified to be President.

The truth, of course, is that it's always the past campaigns that seem substantial and always the current one that doesn't.

"I like Ike" wasn't really what you would call a comprehensive stand on the great issues of the day.

And Harry Truman got elected by promising to "give 'em hell" while George McGovern couldn't get elected even by promising to give everyone in the country a thousand dollars. The difference, it seems, is that Truman was at least smart enough to make it clear that the "em" to whom he was going to give hell were those who weren't going to vote for him no matter what he promised, while McGovern's mistake was that when it became clear that the thousand dollar per voter inducement wasn't working he was not sharp enough to up the bribe.

Nixon made a lot of points with the voters the second time he ran for President by telling them that he had a plan for ending the war in Vietnam and he proved that he had learned his lesson from his first presidential campaign by cleverly avoiding telling anyone what his plan was.

A good number of the nation's leading political scientists have pointed out that when Gerald Ford became President following Nixon's resignation the American people were at first uneasy but then rallied behind Ford when the newspapers carried photos of him operating a pop-up toaster and news reports out of the White House noted that he made his own toast every morning.

A lot of people think that what did in Ford was his pardoning Nixon. Not so. What did in Ford was that he quit making his own toast. People liked the fact that he made his own toast. All the polls showed that. But dumb Jerry Ford got all involved vetoing bills Congress never should have passed, and other things like that which bore the press and the public, and he soon forgot about making his own toast. The rest is history.

Jimmy Carter tried a whole new approach. He bragged that he had a mother who had run off to the Peace Corps at an elderly age and a brother who sat around a gas station all day drinking beer and peeing in places other than the restrooms and a sister who talked to spirits. Some people thought that the fact that Jimmy Carter was less goofy than the rest of his family didn't actually prove that he was qualified to be President of the United States, but apparently most people felt otherwise, at least for awhile.

Ronald Reagan ran two great campaigns, the first one best remembered by his saying "There you go again" every time Carter said something Reagan wished people wouldn't pay attention to and the second one best remembered by his ads saying, "It's morning again in America," which, it appears, is a lot smarter thing to say than, "It's getting dark" or "Night's falling," which, come to think of it, was what his opponents always seemed to be saying, perhaps hoping that a majority of the voters were afraid of the dark (anyone with any sense knows that most Americans are *not* afraid of the dark. Not *real* Americans anyway).

What Jack Newell did was learn from the mistakes and successes of others. He did that the easy way. He just listened to Bill Schulz. And then he followed Schulz's advice. After all, how would a veterinarian know anything about running for President?

Schulz saw to it that Governor Newell was very well briefed throughout the campaign. The candidate was prepared for just about any eventuality. For example, he knew that if anyone asked him how he'd feel if his wife were raped and murdered the smart thing was to stress that he disapproved. Back in 1988 Michael Dukakis had tried a different approach. He had responded to that question by making a passionate plea for calling a hemispheric summit to talk about a different subject. It didn't fly.

Jack Newell also followed George Bush's successful example. That is, he took every possible opportunity to make it very clear that he was pro-American. He also made it quite clear that he was not particularly fond of paying taxes. And he promised that he would not pass out "Get Out Of Jail Free" tickets to hardened criminals.

They campaigned in all the states. They got Jack Newell photographed at all the appropriate national shrines. They proved that he had some tie with each ethnic group. And they took care not to say anything worth remembering during the two televised debates.

It was indeed the perfect campaign.

Probably the comment that was made most often about the campaign was that Jack Newell was saying "the right things." The press frequently quoted people saying that. And the voters apparently concluded that a candidate who was saying the right things must be the right choice.

Nobody paid much attention to Jack Newell's running mate.

That was good.

Because the candidate for Vice President was, as Jack Newell and Bill Schulz came to learn, a real jerk.

Jack Newell carried 44 of the 50 states.

In accordance with the Twelfth Amendment to the Constitution of the United States, so did "The Jerk."

# *Four*

As President, Jack Newell had the qualities the nation needed. But as a human being he had a failing which frequently afflicts persons who are elected to high public office largely on the strength of the imagination and skill of others who showed the way.

He didn't like to be reminded that if it were not for Bill Schulz he wouldn't be President; that if it were not for Schulz he never would have known how to go about running for President; that if it were not for Schulz he never would have even *thought* of running for President.

It wasn't that Schulz ever said such things or even gave any indications that he thought such things. And it wasn't so much that others brought it up. At first they did, right after the election. But not for very long. The truth is, people quickly forgot about Schulz's role. By the time Inauguration Day rolled around there was barely any media attention on Bill Schulz anymore.

Still, much as he liked the man and much as he respected his abilities and his character, Jack Newell had great difficulty handling the fact that he was President of the United States mainly because of Bill Schulz rather than mainly because of himself. He was jealous. And jealousy makes people do strange things. Even to friends.

He called Schulz in one day shortly after the election and asked him to be co-chairman of the Inauguration festivities. When Schulz promptly accepted the honor, the President-elect then told him that he would also consider it a great personal favor if he would accept a "very important" post in the new Administration.

Schulz did not particularly like being offered the position of Director of the United States Information Agency. What he had had in mind was holding a couple of different Cabinet posts during the Newell years. But he assumed that the President's motivation for picking USIA was to have him in Washington in a prestigious position but still relatively free for the more critical task of being the President's behind-the-scenes top advisor. So Schulz made no objection. He suggested no alternative. He simply accepted, thinking things would just sort of go along as they had been going.

It didn't work out that way. For the first several months of the Newell Administration, Schulz was asked to drop by the Oval Office a few times a week for informal chats with the President and his chief of staff or maybe a couple of key Cabinet members. Even after those early days he was included at most of the White House state luncheons and dinners and he remained a fixture on the Washington social scene. But as the months and then a couple of years rolled by he spent less and less time in the private company of the President.

It was very clear to Bill Schulz, and to anyone else who noticed such things, that Jack Newell was making a point of governing without any dependence upon Schulz. But that was a subject the two men never talked about the few times they might have had the opportunity to do so.

The President is the nation's chief executive and Jack Newell was a very competent executive, a born problem-solver. He was keenly intelligent, very hard-working, highly principled, and he had firm convictions and the courage of his convictions. If he had been elected president of Ford Motor Company or DuPont or IBM, or if the people of the country as a whole had as much common sense as do the people of New Hampshire, he would have enjoyed immense popularity and faced no problem whatsoever as re-election time approached. But as time wore on it became very clear that Jack Newell would face considerable difficulty getting re-elected President.

The polls showed him trailing his most likely opponent. They also showed that the Vice President had a significantly higher approval rating.

Jack Newell was competent and he worked hard and he put the country's best interest ahead of his own political interest.

Big mistake.

The public perception that came across was that he was involved in too many controversies. He was seen as harming people because, as portrayed by the media and by his opponents, he seemed too anxious to curtail all sorts of real and imagined benefits.

There was a serious federal deficit to deal with and President Newell proposed serious specific measures for controlling costs, but the decision-makers in Congress opted to postpone such decisions. That is, the decision-makers decided not to make decisions. At least not difficult ones.

Even people who spiritedly denounced over-government had their hands deep into the government's pocket and President Newell pointed out lots of very specific examples of that and then proposed very specific remedies. But the nation's Congressional decision-makers decided to take a pass whenever the President called for such decisions.

The nation's housing program and banking systems and public pensions were national scandals and President Newell studied hard and worked hard and came forth with specific recommendations for getting at the root, not just the symptoms, of the problems. But of the hundreds of decision-makers the people send to Washington, he seemed to stand nearly alone in wanting to just dig in and come to grips with making the truly important decisions. The situation in Washington was so bad, he once remarked to his brother, that if the issue ever came into focus, and if any poll showed that some voters had a strong preference for one while other voters had a strong preference for the other, most Members of Congress would just stand there in line and die of starvation before they could make up their minds whether to order a Big Mac or a Quarter Pounder.

When Congress sent him costly new spending programs without giving any thought to the matter of how to finance them, he sent back thoughtful veto messages. To their constant refrain of "the funds can be found," he patiently and politely pointed out that the funds were not lost. What needed to be found, he said, was some backbone.

To Jack Newell's way of thinking, what the country needed was leaders with political courage. What it was getting, he lamented, was the Little Bo Peep approach to problem-solving—just leave it alone and hope it comes home. The non-politician President just couldn't get it through his head that the last thing most people who aspire to get elected to be the nation's decision-makers want to do is actually make decisions.

It really got to him. To the point that every morning in the shower he found himself singing one of the songs from the old Broadway musical, "1776": *"A second flood, a simple famine, a plague of locust everywhere, I'd accept with some despair, but, no, you sent us Congress, Good God, sir, is that fair?"*

Singing that song made him feel better. Reading the polls didn't. So one day the President decided to do something about it.

He decided to do what any man of great intelligence and extraordinary common sense would do in his situation.

He called in Bill Schulz.

Washingtoniana

# Five

"How could it happen?" asked the President. "I won by one of the biggest landslides ever. Just like Reagan and Bush. Seems like only yesterday. And now look at the mess I'm in."

The President's secretary closed the door behind them and Jack Newell and Bill Schulz were alone in the Oval Office. Schulz didn't respond to the President's opening words. The President motioned him to sit down on one of the two white couches next to the fireplace.

"Heard a new story you'll get a kick out of," said the President, as he sat down on the matching couch opposite Schulz. "It's about that great public servant whom you and I have placed one heartbeat away from the Presidency."

"What'd 'The Jerk' do now?" asked Schulz.

"Heard it in Illinois when I was out there for the Lincoln Day ceremony," said the President. "It was at this private little fundraising party just before we went over to the dinner speech. This little old lady I was presenting a pin to in commemoration of all her years of work for the Party, she's the one who told me . . ."

"Told you what?" asked Schulz.

"Well, the Vice President got his start in politics as sheriff of one of those little redneck counties down in that part of the state . . ."

"I didn't remember that," said Schulz.

"Yeah, Bates was sheriff," said the President. "Anyhow, he's coming into the county jail one night and he's walking past the area where the prisoners come out to talk with their visitors. There's one of the women prisoners cleaning up things in that room late at night and when she spots Bates she shouts out to him: 'Sheriff, Sheriff, I'll need some Kotex in the morning . . .' "

"Kotex?"

"Well, Bates stops dead in his tracks and this dumb look comes over his face," said the President.

"It's still there," said Schulz.

"He turns around and looks at this woman prisoner and shakes his finger at her face . . ."

"Gives her the finger?" asked Schulz.

"No, no, Bill," said the President. "He shakes his finger at her. Then he says, 'What do you think this place is, lady, a resort?' Well, this woman prisoner, she doesn't know what to think. She looks at Bates and says: 'Sheriff, I didn't mean any offense. It's just that most of your help is on vacation and I didn't have anyone else to tell. All I said is that I'll need some Kotex in the morning.' "

The President noticed that Schulz looked puzzled. He decided to speed up the story: "Well, Bates gets mad and shouts at her: 'I told you, lady, this isn't a resort. You can just forget about that Kotex stuff. You'll eat cornflakes just like everybody else.' "

Schulz smiled and chuckled a bit, but he didn't laugh the way the President had hoped he would.

"He probably wasn't joking, Bill," said the President. "Anyhow, you should have seen the look on this little old lady's face when I just split apart laughing. Thank God only a couple of people heard our little chat. And thank God the press had just left the room and didn't see me crack up and come over to find out why."

"Thank God," said Schulz.

"Yeah, good thing they missed this one," said the President. "Because this lady, Bill, she got really pissed when I laughed. You should have seen her. She had this dumbfounded look on her face and she said, 'Mr. President, that isn't funny. Bates wasn't trying to be funny. I'm telling you, Mr. President, the man's the biggest jerk ever to come out of Illinois. I've known him and his goofy family all my life, since way before those fools in the press started treating him like he was hot stuff. Hot stuff, my ass! He's a jerk! That's all Bates is. An incredible jerk! I still can't believe you picked him to be Vice President. You must have been drunk or something. But don't you ever let him become President. Don't you ever let that happen. Hear me, don't you ever let that happen!' "

"This was a little old lady talking to you like that?" asked Schulz.

"Must have been in her early 80's," said the President. "A real character."

"Well," said Schulz, "she obviously has better sense when it comes to picking a vice president than certain other people do."

"Oh, no, you don't," said the President. "I'm not the one who picked 'The Jerk'—you picked him. I didn't even know him. I'd only even heard his name a few times before you picked him."

"I *recommended* him," said Schulz. "You *picked* him."

"That's a distinction without a difference and you know it," said the President.

"Perhaps," said Schulz, "but the history books will say *you* did it. And that's differentiation enough for me."

Vice President Bernie Bates had seemed like a harmless choice. He was, after all, a man who had served in the House of Representatives for some fifteen years. He was popular in his section of Illinois and Schulz had felt that if the election were close, which it did not turn out to be, having someone who was strong in southern Illinois just might tip the balance in that state and Illinois just might tip the balance in the election.

Bates had been no real star. In fact, the word that always seemed to come up about him back when Schulz was screening Vice Presidential possibilities was "average." He was of average looks. Average weight. Average height. And, so it seemed, average intelligence. Even his age, 55, was about average range for those being considered.

Bernie Bates was a politician, pure and simple. It seemed that whenever two or more people gathered for breakfast, lunch or dinner anywhere in southern Illinois, Congressman Bernie Bates would show up. People said that about him— "You can always count on Bernie to make every effort to attend." When called upon for a few remarks, his speech was always mostly about how delighted he was to be there. Whenever he couldn't attend an event he sent a representative who talked about how hard Bates was working for them and he also sent a letter to be read or sometimes, if it was a big enough event, he sent a video tape. A staff photographer followed him everywhere he went and took photos of Bates with anyone and everyone he bumped into.

Back in Washington, the Congressman's staff worked long hours screening the back-home press for anything anyone did that would give Bates an excuse to send that person a personal letter containing profuse congratulatory remarks suitable for framing. The staff wrote all the letters.

Congressman Bernie Bates spent a good part of his working day signing those scores of congratulatory letters. He also answered letters his constituents had sent him. That is, he fixed his name to letters his staff had written for him. He also kept busy by autographing all those photos of himself. And, of course, he met with all sorts of visiting groups, which were always delighted to hear him remark that, deep down, his sympathies were with them. Of course with him, as with many others in public office, there was no deep down. He was not particularly interested in ideas and issues. Like so many of his colleagues, he found it quite annoying to have to be taken away from all this every so often and have to walk over to the floor of the House and cast a vote or two. On the way over to vote an aide or two would accompany him and explain to him who was for and who was against and which was the "safer" way for him to vote. If there was one thing he strongly believed in, it was that it was not a good idea to become identified with anything that very many people might consider controversial.

"What a horrible mistake!" said the President.

"It's no big deal," said Schulz. "Nobody really cares who's Vice President."

"It's a crime that we put this man in the empty suit a heartbeat away from the Presidency," said Jack Newell. "It scares the hell out of me. I have a complete jerk as my Vice President and you tell me it's no big deal. Good grief!"

"There have been jerks as Vice Presidents before," said Bill Schulz. "It's never hurt the country."

"There have been jerks as President," said the President. "And *that* has hurt the country badly."

Bill Schulz leaned forward and looked straight into the President's eyes. "Is the media making any issue of Bates?" he asked. Then he answered his own question: "No." And then he asked another question: "Is there anything in the polls to indicate that he's any part of the reason why you happen to be so down in the polls? Again he answered his own question: "No."

Then he asked still another question: "Is there any danger that Bates could become President?"

Before he could answer that one himself, the President interrupted him and said that the point that he really wanted to get across to Schulz was that it was getting pretty obvious he could not win again. "Maybe I shouldn't even run," said the President. "The polls all show that Bates is more popular with the public than I am. Of course they don't know him like we do. Frightening, isn't it? 'The Jerk' may become President of the United States."

"I think Stupp would win if it were a Bates-Stupp race," said Schulz.

"Oh, that's just wonderful," said the President in his most sarcastic tone. "We shouldn't worry because if the public gets to choose between 'The Jerk' and the airhead they'll probably pick the airhead. That's so reassuring!"

Bill Schulz didn't respond. He stood up from his couch and walked slowly over to the fireplace. He looked at the model ship on the mantel. The plaque on the base identified it as the *HMS Bounty*. It was a beautiful replica, hand-carved and perfectly to scale. Schulz stood there looking it over, admiring the detail. The Oval Office was perfectly quiet for a moment. Then Schulz turned around and glanced down at the President who was still sitting in the nearby couch. The President was looking up at him.

"You didn't ask me over here today after all this time just to tell me that 'The Jerk' is still a jerk and 'The Airhead' is still an airhead," said Schulz. He said it in a tone that sounded almost hostile.

The President of the United States was visibly uncomfortable. Bill Schulz's phrase "after all this time" had shot through him like an arrow. He felt a sharp pain. He felt just awful.

It was out in the open now. Finally out in the open between them. Which meant that the President now had to face up to the unpleasant fact of his ill treatment of his old friend before this conversation could move forward.

"Bill, come sit down," said the President. "I've got something I need to talk with you about. Something I wish I had talked with you about a long time ago."

Schulz moved away from the fireplace and sat down again on the white couch he had been sitting on across from the President's white couch.

The President looked down at his hands for a moment and then he slowly glanced up and looked across the six-foot gap that separated him from Bill Schulz. "The Bible says that pride goeth before the fall," said the President. "Do you know what I'm trying to say?"

"Go on. I'm listening," said Schulz.

"Look," said the President, "we're both thinking the same thing. I've been a damned poor friend to you ever since I became President. That's what you're thinking, isn't it? And I don't blame you for feeling that way. You're right."

"Wouldn't it be better for us to hear what you're thinking rather than speculate on what I might be thinking?" said Schulz.

The President cleared his throat and paused a moment. "What I'm trying to say, Bill, is that I'm sorry. I know I wouldn't be President if it hadn't been for you. I guess I'm more vain than I thought. I guess my ego just wouldn't accept it. I guess I became jealous that the real credit for my making it here rightly belongs to you rather than to me. Maybe it's because I came into this office so in awe of it all that it went to my head. Do you know what I mean?"

"I'm listening," said Schulz.

"It is hard to be President and still be humble," said the President. "It really is. You get up one morning and you take a ride up to Capitol Hill and take an oath and give a speech and then watch a parade and go to some parties and all of a sudden from then on you are the center of the world. Everyone treats you like you're a living legend or something. You start accepting it. It's hard for anyone who hasn't been President to know what it's like to spend so many of your waking hours thinking about what history is going to say about you."

"It's going to say that you treated your best friend like shit," joked Schulz.

The President laughed. So did Bill Schulz.

"Someday, someway, somehow," said the President, "I am going to make it all up to you. Whatever it takes. Mark my word."

Schulz looked across at the President. He suddenly felt sorry for his old friend. The laugh that was there a moment ago had gone off to that secret place that laughs go after they have performed their task. The President looked dejected. He looked like a man who had just lost his best friend. "There's something I should say," said Schulz. "I'm very proud to be your friend. I want you to know that."

"Thanks, I appreciate that," said the President. "I really do. More than you realize."

"Look, I could see what was happening," said Schulz, "and, sure, I resented it. It hurt. It made me angry."

"I'm sorry," said the President.

"Jack, ah, sorry, Mr. President . . ."

"It's 'Jack,' Bill, for you it's 'Jack.' "

"Jack, I wish I had been here, at the White House, helping you each day," said Schulz. "If you had been listening to me instead of to whomever the hell it is who gives you political advice these days, well, I don't think you'd be getting the crap kicked out of you in the polls. I know that sounds a bit cocky, but, shit, it's the truth."

"Bill, it's not that anyone has replaced what you used to do," said the President. "I guess I just sort of made it a point not to have any special political advisor. I guess I was vain enough to want to do it without your help."

"You probably think it was smart of Custer not to have reinforcements," said Schulz. "But let me finish. What I want to tell you is why I thought you should be President, why I think you have been an outstanding President."

"Well, thanks, Bill, I appreciate that," said the President.

"You're a good man," said Schulz. "A truly remarkable person in the political arena. You're honest as they come. You've got character. Good moral character. You've got a fine mind. You're conscientious. You're responsible. You're a man of principle. And you really care. You really care about our country. You have put America's interest above your own political interest. You're a true patriot."

"Thanks, Bill, I . . ."

"I'm not finished," said Schulz. "I don't think you under-stand—I think you sense it, but I don't think you fully com-prehend it. You really don't understand just how rare these qualities are in public life today. Especially courage. Hell, I guess I forgot to mention courage. Shows just how rare it is these days. But you've got courage. Genuine moral courage. You don't just take the easy path. You're willing to try to blaze a new trail. You're willing to put your own convenience and political future at risk for the sake of principle. Time and time again. That's, well, that's what almost all the others lack. You're a man of principle and courage in a field that is overrun with chickens and cowards and wimps. That's why I busted my butt to get you elected."

"Thanks, Bill," said the President.

"Hey, I'll admit it," said Schulz, "it's only human nature. I was certainly hoping in the back of my mind for some personal gain out of it. More interesting horizons in life. But that was secondary. Honest, it was. Deep down, corny as it may sound, I sincerely felt that what I was doing was good for the country. I felt patriotic about it. I still do."

"And now how do you feel, Bill?" asked the President. "How do you feel after this good man, this man of character and courage, responded to all that you did for him by being embarrassed about it because it reminded him of his own limitations? How do you feel about the way he responded to your friendship and commitment by excluding you from playing the part you should have been playing in his Presidency?"

"I guess I wouldn't list loyalty as your strongest suit," said Schulz. Bill Schulz smiled as he said that. The President didn't.

"I pride myself on loyalty," said the President. "That's one of the reasons I feel like such a shit about the way things have gone. I meant what I said a moment ago. Someday, someway, I'll atone. I truly mean that. But for now I just hope we can put it behind us . . ."

"Of course," said Schulz.

"And go back to the way things used to be," continued the President.

"That'd be wonderful," said Schulz.

"Bill, the reason I asked you here today was to tell you I'm sorry and to try to get things right between us," said the

President. "I know I should have done it long ago. I hope it's not too late."

"Let's forget it was ever necessary," said Bill Schulz.

"I need your help, Bill," said the President. "The situation is just awful. If I don't run for re-election, the next President of the United States is certain to be either that jerk Bates or that airhead actor Herb Stupp. And if I do run, well, it's probably certain to be the airhead. That clown is leading me by 14 points in the polls and he's nothing but a damned television actor."

Herb Stupp was a bit more than merely "a damned television actor." Not a whole lot more, but a little bit more. He was also a political activist.

Like many in Hollywood, Stupp had long ago found it very helpful to his career to sign up with the Hollywood fringe groups and be a spokesman for all sorts of "worthy" causes. He oozed credibility. He had jet black hair and ocean blue eyes and he was handsome without being pretty-boy. He was tall and he looked strong. And his voice was deep and pleasant to listen to. He came across as warm and friendly.

Pushed on by his activist friends, Herb Stupp had received enormous publicity and praise as a result of his "willingness to speak out" in favor of "clean air" and "clean water" and "fairness" and "better opportunities for all Americans." He testified before Congress several times, talking about "concerns" that had been the subjects of some of the television shows. Every time he did so a large number of Senators and Members of the House of Representatives fell all over him and got their pictures taken with him to put in their newsletters so voters would know that they had crossed paths with a real star. He was always treated in a far more deferential manner than that accorded to witnesses who know much about the subject they were talking about. He had once spent a night sleeping on a Los Angeles sidewalk with some homeless people. It had not occurred to him, or to any of the news media reporters covering that "consciousness-raising event," that it might have been even more fun, at least for the homeless, if he had simply invited some of those unfortunate people to come over to his place for dinner and spend the night in some of the many empty rooms in his huge Hollywood mansion.

"Can you believe it?" asked the President.

"Believe what?" asked Schulz.

"A damned television actor!" said the President. "That guy Stupp is nothing but a second-rate actor and he's got the nomination locked-up and he's clobbering me in the polls."

"He was the star of a big hit series," said Schulz.

"Somebody told me the other day that Stupp once appeared in a commercial for dog food," said the President. "A dog food commercial! Can you believe that? A pitchman for dog food running for President of the United States!"

"He hasn't done a dog food commercial in years," said Schulz.

"He used to," said the President. "Think about that. How would that sound in the history books?"

"Like a humble beginning," said Schulz.

The President couldn't resist smiling at that one. "And as if things weren't complicated enough already, Bill, I really don't see how I could in good conscience recommend that jerk Bates as my running mate if I did run, knowing what we know now. But how could I dump him without making my own situation even worse? I don't think I could pull it off. And if I tried to dump him and failed, well, that would be even worse, wouldn't it?"

"That would be catastrophic," said Schulz.

"Exactly," said the President. "But if I explained to the public how bizarre he really is, well, that might just hurt me worse still."

"Probably," said Schulz. "You'd be telling the public that you don't have confidence in your own judgement, that you've been misleading them about Bates for nearly four years now. At least that's the spin your critics would put on it."

"There's even the possibility," said the President, "that he has more clout in the Party than I do right now and it may come down to our Party demanding that I step aside in favor of him." The President looked straight into Schulz's eyes: "Can you think of a worse mess I could have gotten myself into?"

Bill Schulz didn't say anything. "Well?" said the President.

"Well, what?" asked Schulz.

"You've got to straighten it out, Bill. You've got to put Humpty Dumpty back together again."

"What are my restrictions?" asked Schulz.

"Just do what you have to do," said the President. "Whatever it takes. As long as it's legal, as long as it's moral, as long as it's ethical, I don't give a shit what kind of cockamamie ideas you come up with. I'm desperate. I'll try anything."

"Anything?" asked Schulz.

"Anything," said the President of the United States.

# Six

One thousand one hundred forty-seven miles from the White House, as the crow flies southwest, in the little town of Freka, Arkansas, Hank Harrison was sitting at the breakfast table, eating two eggs sunnyside up, a slice of ham and his usual heaping pile of hominy grits. He was also reading *The Arkansas Democrat-Gazette*.

"Golly, golly," he kept murmuring.

Mattie-Faye, Hank's wife of thirty-one years, had long since given up asking Hank what it was in the morning newspapers that brought on his daily murmurings of "golly, golly" at the breakfast table.

Every morning after he awoke and then showered, shaved and dressed, Hank walked the half-mile from his modest three bedroom brick house to George Smith's drugstore in Freka's little shopping center to pick up his copy of the Little Rock newspaper. He prefered to do this rather than have the newspaper delivered to his door because he thought it was a good idea to force himself to get a little exercise every morning. He prided himself on the fact that he never missed a day of reading the state's leading newspaper. He also regularly read *The Fayetteville Northwest Arkansas Times*, an evening newspaper.

Although Hank had been born and raised in the Freka area—about thirty-five miles northeast of Fayetteville and some ten miles southeast of Berryville—he was quite different from what most people usually imagine a resident of an Ozark area town with a population of 976 to be. What made him so different was his reading. Hank Harrison read just about anything he could get his hands on. Especially anything about history or government or politics or current events.

"Show me a reader and I'll show you a leader," his mother had inculcated into Hank when he was a child. Most so-called "leaders" read much less than Hank did.

He was exceptionally smart. And extraordinarily well informed.

He looked like a hick.

Tall and lanky, the 57-year-old Hank had a fondness for dressing in a way that made him appear as if he had just stepped out of an old *Li'l Abner* comic strip. Like those goofy overalls that always looked a size too big for him. He even dressed a bit like a cartoon character on Sundays when he and Mattie-Faye attended young Reverend Ralph Kinney Bennett's First Bible Baptist Church, formerly South Street Baptist Church. ("A going church for a coming Savior," proclaimed the sign at the front entrance).

Townsfolk said you could recognize Hank two blocks away, not just because of his height and thin frame, but also because of his thick silvery gray hair which, some swore, sparkled in the dark. His face was even proportionally more thin than the rest of him and the dark tan he always carried covered a more than normal supply of wrinkles for a man his age. He was, as Mattie-Faye liked to say, "as handsome as Abraham Lincoln must have been before he grew that beard."

Most people in Freka dressed like normal middle Americans, of course, but it appealed to Hank's unusually dry sense of humor to go around looking like the Hollywood stereotype of an Ozark hick. So he often wore plaid shirts with striped ties and he was rarely seen without his straw hat that always looked like it had just been trampled on.

Hank Harrison was different. Not just that he was smarter than most people. Not just that he was so widely read and well informed. Not just that he seemed to sort of balance or compensate for his more intellectual tastes by looking the part of a hick. Not just all that.

What also distinguished Hank Harrison from most of the other townsfolks of Freka, Arkansas, was what Mattie-Faye liked to refer to as, a bit sarcastically, his "presidential heritage."

It seems that when Hank was attending high school up in Berryville, he knew more about history and government, especially American history and American government, and current events, too, than just about anyone who had ever attended the school—and he also knew more about those subjects than anyone then teaching there. He was especially interested in biographies of the Presidents.

So it was probably inevitable that sooner or later he would read up on William Henry Harrison. He would never forget the day it happened. He was sitting in the living room of the family farmhouse one evening reading a history book and he was chuckling, "Golly, golly. Now ain't that just like a Harrison. Golly, ain't that just like a Harrison."

His father finally inquired about what it was that he kept talking to himself about. So Hank explained: "This fella's whole reputation was built on a victory at a battle which no respectable historian considers much of a military victory at all. Then he goes and gets himself nominated for President of the United States. Any special qualifications? No. Just that battle that really wasn't much of a battle at all. But he gets nominated. Because most of the other fellas have so many enemies and he doesn't."

His father stopped what he was doing and listened carefully. "He doesn't win, but he does OK," said Hank. "So they run him again the next time. Doesn't even really have a platform, just a couple of silly slogans. But—zap!—he beats an incumbent. I just think it's kinda funny."

"You talking about who I think you're talking about?" asked his father.

"William Henry Harrison," said Hank.

"Well you better not let your Uncle Gaines hear ya say nothin against him," said his father.

And that is when, for the first time, Hank Harrison learned that his Uncle Gaines claimed to have found evidence, while researching the family tree, that he and Hank's father, and, of course, Hank and his brothers and sisters and cousins, were descendants of the two Harrison presidents—William Henry and Benjamin.

Not many people would put much stock in Uncle Gaines' abilities as a researcher, but everyone in the family did know that the Harrisons did come from Virginia originally and that they had lived in Ohio before eventually moving on to Arkansas—and William Henry Harrison was born in Virginia and did later move to Ohio, and his grandson, Benjamin, was born and raised in Ohio.

What puzzled Hank was that, as best he knew, Uncle Gaines had mentioned his "discovery" only to Hank's father, and neither he nor, as best he knew, anyone else, had ever been informed of it until that day Hank just happened to be reading about the first Harrison president and had made some comments about him. Hank could never understand it: his father didn't seem to give a damn if they were really descendants of the Harrison presidents.

"But don't you think it's kinda special that you and I are descendants of two presidents?" Hank asked his father.

"Any fool can be a descendant. The important thing in life is being a good ancestor," replied Hank's father.

"But why did you never mention it before?" asked Hank. "If you don't think it's important, don't you at least think it's interesting?"

"Maybe," said his father.

"Are you and Uncle Gaines the only ones who know this?" asked Hank.

"I think so," said his father, "but I'm not sure. I think we might have mentioned it to your mother and your aunt Linda."

"How come ya'll never mentioned it to me or anyone else in the family?" asked Hank.

Hank's father set aside the magazine he was reading and he looked at Hank and then quietly said: "I guess we were just kinda ashamed that the Harrisons have produced only two Presidents. That makes us no better than them Yankee Adams folks. So there's really not that much to brag about, is there?"

It was the sort of statement that the old boy loved to make. The good-natured grin that flashed on his face gave away the fact that he wasn't really as silly as such statement as this, which he often came out with, might make him appear to someone who didn't know him and didn't notice his give-away grin.

From the day of that incident, Hank made a great point of studying the history of the Harrison presidents. He could tell you every good point that anyone had ever attributed to either one of them. He could speak at great length about their ac-complishments. And when he talked of them, which he did much more often than anyone cared to listen to, he spoke in a tone of utmost respect, almost awe. Never again did Hank refer to William Henry Harrison's military victory at Tippe-canoe as "not much of a battle" or reiterate his early impres-sion that the man had not been particularly well qualified to be president.

His father's disparaging remarks about the insignificance of descendants' claim to fame aside, Hank let it be known to anyone who would listen that he and his family were descen-dants of not just one, but two, presidents of the United States.

He convinced himself that having presidential blood in your veins—"especially a double dose"—carried with it some serious responsibility to your offspring. And one such re-sponsibility, as he saw it (he couldn't disagree more with his father's indifference) was to know all he could about his famous presidential ancestors and also as much as he could about their field—government and politics.

That's why throughout his life Hank almost religiously kept up with government and politics and current events. He subscribed to *The Washington Post* and *The New York Times* and *The Wall Street Journal*. He subscribed to every major newsmagazine and opinion journal, including *National Review* and *The New Republic*. He even read *Human Events* and *The National Journal*. And over the years he had amassed a personal library that would put most college presidents to shame.

He had tried to get as good an education as he could. He attended the University of Arkansas on a scholarship but he had left after one year when his father took ill and everyone just sort of agreed that he seemed the best choice to step in and run the family farm. He ran it for years before finally giving it up to buy the dry-cleaning store in town. When he bought that business, he and Mattie-Faye moved into their modest house in Freka.

Not a day went by in the dry-cleaning store but that Hank paused to ponder, if only for a moment, the fact that he carried that "double dose of presidential blood" in his veins. He remembered what his father had said about trying to be a good ancestor rather than just a descendant, but, dammit, he just couldn't help himself—he felt there was something special about it.

Not that he had any great desire to run for public office himself or anything like that. The way he saw it, anyone who came from presidential stock should not run for local office. There was just something, well, inappropriate about it. To his way of thinking, someone from presidential stock shouldn't even run for the state legislature or even the House of Representatives (the Senate would be alright)—unless he honestly felt that the timing was right to parlay it all the way to a crack at the big prize itself, the Presidency.

Long ago Hank had concluded that this was not to be his destiny. Nothing even remotely approaching an opportunity for him to pursue a political career had ever come along. His destiny, he had concluded, was to wait patiently and hope that when the political call returned to the Harrison family it would summon one of his sons or his daughter or one of his grandchildren and he would live to see the Presidency of the third Harrison.

And that would show those Adams folks just who's tops!

In the meantime, well, he would just enjoy life in Freka, making a decent living operating the town's only dry-cleaning business, which attracted customers from miles around, and raising his family and living among people who, for whatever their minor faults and lack of interest in the Harrison presidents, were as good as the human race turns out.

"Golly, golly," Hank kept murmuring to himself. Mattie-Faye looked up and just shook her head. They were eating breakfast at the same time President Newell and Bill Schulz were having coffee together at the White House. In both places the topic of conversation was the President's political fate.

"Mattie-Faye," said Hank, "I just can't understand why this Stupp fella is so popular around here. He isn't really saying anything."

"He's in the papers everyday," said Mattie-Faye, "and on radio and television all the time, too."

"I know that," said Hank. "What I mean is, he uses lots of words, and they sound nice, but when you try to put them together they don't add up to any ideas."

"You know he's got ideas, Hank," said Mattie-Faye. "Everybody does."

"I'm not so sure," said Hank. "I have read just about everything Stupp has said and just about everything that's been written about him."

"I'm sure you have," said Mattie-Faye.

"Well," said Hank, "if there's a constructive new idea there, or even an old one for that matter, I just don't see it. All this guy is doing is stringing a bunch of slogans together."

"Folks do seem to get a chuckle from his slogan," said Mattie-Faye. "You've got to admit that. And you can't say the President is good for many chuckles."

"Mattie-Faye, that is the silliest slogan for a candidate for President of the United States that I have ever heard." As he said that, Hank noticed a photo of Herb Stupp in *The Arkansas Democrat-Gazette*. In the background behind the candidate he could see the Stupp slogan: *"WE NEED A PRESIDENT WHO CAN ACT."*

"You should talk about silly slogans, Hank Harrison," said Mattie-Faye. "Of all people, fella, you should talk."

"What do you mean?" asked Hank.

"You know what I mean," said Mattie-Faye. "That President relative of yours, however he's related to ya'll Harrisons. I've read one of those books of yours about him."

"Really?" said Hank.

"Yeah, really," said Mattie-Faye. "All he ever did, from what I could tell, is run around the country spouting silly slogans."

"William Henry was a fine President, and history would have had a great deal to say about him if he hadn't died a month after he took office," said Hank.

"Only President ever to get killed by being inaugurated," said Mattie-Faye. "What a pathetic claim to fame!"

"He caught a bad cold, Mattie-Faye," said Hank. "Came down with pneumonia. That can happen."

"Didn't know enough to come in out of the rain," said Mattie-Faye. "Silly fool just stood there in the pouring rain and rambled on and on and never said one sentence in his entire Inaugural address that anyone ever remembered anyhow. Like I said, only President ever to get killed by being inaugurated. And you wonder why your father and mother never liked to talk about him."

"He was a fine man, Mattie-Faye, you know that."

"Now, Hank," said Mattie-Faye, "if the fella wasn't related to ya'll's family somehow, you—of all people, you—would know it's kinda ridiculous that the guy got elected by doing nothing more than dancing around the country, him and his fool friends, singing 'Tippecanoe and Tyler, Too' and 'Van, Van's a Used-Up Man.' Talk about silly slogans! Don't have any point to them. Not that I can see."

"The point is, Mattie-Faye, maybe you think this Stupp fella is cute or something," said Hank, "but he's just not saying anything that anyone with a lick of sense should find worth listening to. Now the President, if you really study things, says a lot of intelligent things. The problem is, nobody seems to listen to what he is really saying."

"You know as well as I do, Hank, that Herb Stupp is as good as elected our next President," said Mattie-Faye.

"I hope not," said Hank. "It looks like it. But I hope not."

"Well, you tell me, Hank, you know so much about all that kinda stuff, you tell me what the President can do to keep Herb Stupp from beating him," said Mattie-Faye. "You tell me, you know so much. Come on, you tell me."

"I can't think of what he could do," said Hank, "but I sure hope he's got some smart advisors who can come up with some good ideas."

"They'd better do it real quick," said Mattie-Faye.

# Seven

To Bill Schulz, it all came down to a pretty obvious and relatively simple public relations problem that ought not to be particularly difficult to solve.

No question about it, Herb Stupp's public relations efforts had been excellent. People knew him. People liked him. No great controversies surrounded him or attached themselves to him. Conservatives thought of him as reasonably sympathetic to them. Liberals thought of him as reasonably sympathetic to them. People who liked to think of themselves as not tied to any political philosophy thought of him as, well, one of them. Pretty good p.r.

But to Schulz's way of thinking, the success of Stupp's public relations campaign was largely attributable to dumb luck. It was working so well principally because it was pitted against such a poor p.r. campaign on the part of the President. The President's p.r. campaign was, in fact, just about non-existent, little more to it than periodically dismissing Herb Stupp's activities as "public relations gimmicks."

To Bill Schulz, this was dumb. Incredibly dumb. Of course the things that Stupp was doing were public relations gimmicks! What did they think a presidential campaign is all about! It's your gimmicks versus their gimmicks. Whoever has the best gimmicks wins. Simple.

At their next meeting in the Oval Office, Schulz laid before the President his preliminary ideas for salvaging the Presidency for Jack Newell.

"The basic problem," Schulz told the President, "is that in the mind of the average American your Presidency can be summed up in two four-letter words."

The President looked at Schulz with a puzzled expression. "Four-letter words?"

"Dull and cold," said Bill Schulz.

"I'm dull and I'm cold, huh?" said the President.

"No," said Schulz, "you're not. But people think you are."

"So they're wrong," said the President.

"Doesn't matter whether they're wrong or not," said Schulz. "The only thing that matters is what their perception is. And they are not going to vote for someone they perceive that way."

"So what are you going to do?" asked the President. "Turn me into a man of pizzazz and warmth?"

"In the minds of the voters, yes," said Schulz.

"Good grief," said the President.

"What we have to do," said Schulz, "is have you start coming across as more like a regular guy."

"Just one of the guys, huh?" said the President.

"Man of the people," said Schulz.

"This is goofy, Bill. Come on, I am President of the United States. People expect a certain decorum, a certain dignity and respect for the office."

"Yeah, they do," said Schulz. "A certain amount. But not so damn much! Not all work and no play. Not such extreme business-like performance."

"You saying that people don't want competence?" asked the President. "You saying it doesn't matter?"

"People want to be able to identify with their President," said Schulz. "Like they do with a friend or neighbor. They don't give a crap if their friends and neighbors are competent at their jobs, except, of course, if they happen to work with them, but they do care if they are warm people and enjoyable to be with."

"I've got to be fun?" asked the President. "You have to be fun to be President?"

"Not exactly fun," said Schulz. "Just more enjoyable than you've been. The point is, you have to make people more comfortable with you. That's the key. I know you don't like it. Deep down, I don't like it either. But it's a fact of political life. You go with the flow—or you drown."

"And how do we convince the American people that I'm an OK guy?" asked the President.

"We're going to begin the image restoration by having you do some little things which are perfectly normal, perfectly uneventful, when done by normal people—but unusual and eventful if *you* do them because *you* happen to be President of the United States," said Schulz. "That's the idea. Very simple. But very effective."

"What sort of things?" asked the President.

"I want you to roll down the window of the Presidential limousine and cuss out some lousy driver," said Schulz.

"What!" said the President.

"It'll be the lead story on all three networks," said Schulz. "I guarantee it. And a big front-page photo in every major newspaper in the country. Makes you human. It's something everybody identifies with."

"You want me to swear at some lousy driver? Don't you think that'd create a big controversy and offend a lot of voters?" asked the President.

"No, no, not swear," said Schulz. "You know, just tell the guy off."

"Bill, I am President. Other cars don't get very close to the President's car."

"We'll get one close enough," said Schulz.

"You'd stage it?" asked the President.

"The world's a stage," said Schulz. "Like I said, you'll get fantastic publicity. I guarantee it. All three networks. Lead story on CNN every hour on the hour for 12 hours. Over and over and over. And a big front page photo and story in every major newspaper in the country. Then all the newsmagazines. Plus you'll be the talk of the talk shows."

"I'm going to be re-elected because I tell off some lousy driver?" said the President. "Come on."

"Don't be a wise-ass, Jack," said Schulz. "That's only one thing in a series of nice little events, the cumulative effect of which will be to make you a warmer and more interesting guy in the minds of the voters."

"You are unbelievable," said the President. "Unbelievable!"

"Let's have you 'accidentally' walk into the area of the White House where they conduct those tours while one of them is going on," said Schulz. "You'll be dripping some. Just stepped out of the shower. You'll have a towel wrapped around your waist. Nothing else on. Then you'll say, 'Whoops, sorry, I took the wrong turn. I was just freshening up for this important luncheon today.' Then you shake a couple of hands while some tourist with a camera snaps a shot."

"And what if none of them has a camera, or shouldn't I ask that?" said the President.

"Those tourists will go bonkers," said Schulz. "They'll be all over the evening news. Telling the country what a regular guy you are. The news media will eat it up. Guarantee it, lead story."

"Yeah, I know," said the President. "All three networks. And front page in every major newspaper in the country."

"Exactly," said Schulz.

"Why?" asked the President.

"You know why," said Schulz. "Because you happen to be President of the United States. That's why. Neat, huh?"

"It's such bullshit," said the President.

"It's what people like," said Schulz.

"So this is the modern day version of giving them bread and circuses?" asked the President. "That what you're saying? This what we have come to?"

Schulz ignored the remark. "We'll do lots of these sorts of things," he continued, "and it'll work wonders. Like next time you go away for the weekend, don't shave. Then let the photographers catch you. That sort of stuff."

The President shook his head slowly and a look of disbelief covered his face: "People are going to judge whether or not I am worthy to be President of the United States on the basis of whether I tell off some driver? Or forget to shave one time? Or talk to tourists while I'm dripping wet and wearing only a towel? That's nutty. Really nutty."

"Isn't it though?" said Bill Schulz.

"It reminds me of when Lyndon Johnson used to make a big show of saving money and conserving energy by running around the White House at night and turning off the lights," said the President.

"Exactly," said Schulz.

"That was such bullshit," said the President.

"It was," said Schulz. "Damn good bullshit. People love that crap. Damned few people stopped and asked themselves why the President of the United States didn't have something better to occupy his time than turning off lightbulbs. People didn't stop and wonder what the help was doing while Lyndon was running around wasting his time performing one of the little tasks that White House servants get paid to perform. People didn't stop and think that the son-of-a-bitch was bankrupting the country with his half-baked spending programs while he was bragging about saving a nickel or two on the White House electric bill."

"That's exactly what I thought at the time," said the President.

"You and maybe six other people," said Schulz. "You're missing the point. The point is, most people don't think. The reason there's so much bullshit in politics is that bullshit works."

"This is awful," said the President.

"Of course it is," said Schulz. "And when was Gerald Ford most popular with the American people? When he was making all those wise and necessary vetoes? Did people give a shit that he had the backbone to stand up for fiscal responsibility? Of course not."

"Yeah, yeah," said the President, "I know. I've heard you before. He shouldn't have quit making his own breakfast."

"Exactly," said Schulz. "The public loved those pictures of him acting like a short-order cook."

"And Jimmy Carter used to carry his own luggage," said the President.

"And the media and the public ate up every bit of that crap, didn't they?" said Schulz.

"They both lost, Bill," said the President. "Ford and Carter both lost. And Johnson would have, too, if he had run again. What does that say for your theory that bullshit guarantees success in presidential politics."

"I didn't say or imply that bullshit guarantees success in presidential politics," said Schulz. "What I'm saying is that failure to come up with some pretty good bullshit guarantees failure in presidential politics. That's what we've been talking about. You've failed to come up with any really good bullshit ever since you became President. And now we're going to remedy that."

"Poor Jerry Ford," said the President.

"What?" asked Schulz.

"Oh, I was thinking about Ford's getting beat," said the President. "Poor bastard. That damn pardon did him in. There was really no alternative. He had to do it. It was the best thing for the country. But people didn't understand that, did they? And it gave the election to Carter. I guess there was just nothing Ford could possibly have done that could have taken away the sting of that pardon."

"Wrong," said Schulz. "With some imaginative p.r. Gerald Ford could have overcome the pardon problem and buried Carter."

"Bull," said the President.

"He could have issued another pardon," said Schulz.

"Another pardon?" asked the President.

"Sure, he should have pardoned Carter," said Schulz.

"Pardoned Carter!" What the hell are you talking about? Pardoned Carter for what?"

"For the same thing he pardoned Nixon for," said Schulz.

"Huh?" said the President.

"For any crimes that he *might* have committed," said Schulz. "That's what Ford pardoned Nixon for. Any crimes that he *might* have committed. He should have pardoned Carter for the same thing. That would have confused enough people to enable Ford to defeat Carter."

"You're mad," said the President.

"What Ford should have done," said Schulz, "is issue a news release announcing that he had pardoned Carter. Just issue it. Just print up a news release and then set copies out in the press room and go hide and wait. That's very important. Be unavailable for comment for awhile. Very important to the scheme. Every news outlet would have had to run with it. Know why? Because every damned one of them would be afraid—terrified!—that one of the others would use it and they'd be scooped. Works every time. The news media is the most predictable group in America. Also the most gullible. It would have been big news. Really big news. All Carter would have been able to say in response is that he didn't do anything that he needed to be pardoned for. He would have been all over the news denying that he had done anything wrong. Think about it. You know how awful that sounds! All you have to do is be seen on television denying that you're guilty of anything and right away everybody thinks you're guilty as sin. But it's the only thing Carter could have done. He could not have avoided it. Absolutely could not have avoided it. Would have finished him off."

"And what could Ford have said when the media finally caught up to him and asked what kind of crap he was pulling?" asked the President.

"Easy," said Schulz. "All Ford would have had to say is: 'Oh, sure, Carter claims that he didn't do anything wrong. Well, that's what Nixon said, too, when I pardoned him.' "

Washingtoniana

"Crazy," said the President. "You're crazy."

"And the American people would have said to themselves, 'Hey, that's right.' I'm telling you, Jack, it would have turned the election right there."

"Bill, what you are really saying is that substance doesn't matter for much . . ."

"Yeah," said Schulz.

"And that competence doesn't matter for much."

"Yeah," said Schulz.

"You can't be that cynical," said the President. "You can't be that damned cynical."

"Can if I want," said Schulz.

"Well, said the President, "I happen to believe that Lincoln was right when he said that you can fool some of the people all of the time and you can fool all of the people some of the time, but you can't fool all of the people all of the time."

"Of course he was right," said Schulz, "as far as he went."

"What do you mean, 'as far as he went'?" asked the President.

Bill Schulz looked at the President. And then he smiled. "In politics, my friend, you only have to fool a majority. And only on special occasions—like elections."

# Eight

Jack Newell started performing the little gimmicks that Bill Schulz recommended. He performed them well.

And it worked.

It's not that the polls turned around overnight, but encouraging signs soon began to appear. Buried in the cross tabs of the polling data, those reams of questions and answers containing information about perceptions, where pollsters delve to discover the "whys" behind the "whats," there was clear evidence of a softening in voter perception about Jack Newell.

Most persons who had previously responded negatively to any suggestion that the President was "a person with the same cares and concerns and feelings that I have" or "the sort of person who reminds me of a close friend or nice neighbor" were now uncertain rather than negative. And most people who previously were uncertain were now inclined positively toward the President.

Phase I of the image make-over was going just as Bill Schulz had thought it would. It was now time for Phase II. And so once again Schulz sat down in the Oval Office alone with the President and dished out another prescription for treating Jack Newell's ill image.

The President of the United States shook his head and rolled his eyes. "That's the nuttiest damned idea I've ever heard," he said.

Schulz was not discouraged. He enthusiastically defended his suggestion that the President become a contestant on *Wheel of Fortune*. "The 'regular guy' campaign is starting to work," Schulz told the President. "What we need to do next is get you lots of television exposure outside the context of your presidential duties. Things that project you as someone people will want to root for."

Jack Newell again shook his head. "The President of the United States as a contestant on *Wheel of Fortune?* I can't believe this is what you've thought of."

"Great, huh?" said Schulz.

"It sounds loony," said the President.

"They'd kill to get you on that show," said Schulz.

"I wasn't suggesting that it would be loony of them," said the President. "It'd be, well, not appropriate for me, as President."

"Why not?" asked Schulz.

"You know why not," said the President.

"It's one hell of an idea," said Schulz. "Who could possibly object?"

"The sponsors of any competing shows, to name just a few," said the President.

"Everybody would watch," said Schulz. "Everybody! The papers would be full of photos of you and Vanna . . ."

"Who?" asked the President.

"Vanna. Vanna White. The gal who turns over the letters."

"Oh, yeah," said the President. "I read somewhere that she gets paid three times as much just to turn those letters as we pay a Member of Congress."

"She does ten times as good a job," said Schulz. "Can you imagine what would happen to that show if they had a bunch of Congressmen turning over those letters? I'd hate to think of it. They'd never get it right."

"I don't know about this one, Bill," said the President. "I know I told you I'd be willing to go along with just about anything you came up with. I mean, I do have total confidence in you, but, holy shit, this is something I never would have imagined."

"People will love it," said Schulz. "And you'll reach —and impress—an audience you just couldn't otherwise make effective contact with. The people on the show and the other contestants will fall all over you. They'll talk about it for weeks. The whole country will talk about it for weeks."

"What if I won?" asked the President.

"Give the prizes to charity," said Schulz. "Don't worry about winning. Hell, it'd make you look smart."

"Then what if I didn't win?" asked the President.

"It'd make you look like a good sport," said Schulz. "Going on there and risking not winning."

"Like a regular guy, huh?" said the President.

"Exactly," said Schulz.

"This is really nutty," said the President. "What would I say while I was on the show?"

"We'll think of things," said Schulz. "We'll do rehearsals. And I'm sure the *Wheel of Fortune* people would be delighted to work with us on it. It'd just be light talk. Friendly stuff. Neighborly."

"Really nutty," said the President.

"No serious stuff," said Schulz. "Just poke some fun at yourself. Maybe say a guy with a job like yours that comes up for renewal in a few months has to think ahead and if that actor guy—call him that, 'that actor guy'—ever got elected, well, maybe you might want to enter his old field—television—and maybe they should consider this an audition. That kinda thing. People will get a kick out of it. They'll love it."

"But what about the fact that other programs might get pissed about my singling out *Wheel of Fortune*?" asked the President.

"I've thought of that," said Schulz, "and the answer is that we are going to have you go on lots of programs, not just *Wheel of Fortune*."

"Shit," said the President.

"Another show you should go on is *Jeopardy!*" said Schulz.

"That's the one where they give you the answer and you have to state the question?" asked the President.

"Right," said Schulz.

"And they get pissed if you don't phrase your answer as a question," asked the President.

"Right," said Schulz.

"That's asinine," said the President.

"Lots of people watch it," said Schulz. "A hell of a lot more than have ever watched a State of the Union Address."

"Why don't they just ask questions and have the contestants give answers?" asked the President. "Why do they do it backwards?"

"How the hell should I know?" said Schulz.

"I thought you knew these sort of things," said the President.

"We'll hit some of the soap operas, too," said Schulz.

"Ah, shit!" said the President.

"It's an audience whose undivided attention no President has ever received," said Schulz.

"Who watches that junk?" asked the President.

"Voters," said Schulz. "Voters."

"How about if I quarterback one of the NFL games while I'm at it?" said the President.

Schulz ignored the sarcasm. "*Cheers* would be a good show to get you on," he said. "They like having celebrity guests. Tip O'Neill was on it once. Gary Hart was on it. The Chairman of the Joint Chiefs of Staff was on it."

"That one would be kinda fun," said the President. "But I'm not going on *Jeopardy!*"

"Why not?" asked Schulz.

"It's too damned difficult," said the President.

"OK," said Schulz. "But we've got to do those daytime shows. You know, *Oprah Winfrey* and *Donahue*. *Regis & Kathie Lee*. *Good Morning America*. *The Today Show*. *Maury Povich*. *The Price Is Right*. All those sorts of shows."

"How do people find the time to watch that stuff?" asked the President.

"Not everybody is President," said Schulz. "And you should do some of the lesser known ones, too. You know, the shows where they talk about cooking and gardening. Nice things like that. Bring a recipe from the White House. A nice simple one. Mix it up right there on the show. It'll be great. Little old ladies all across the country will be making it and implying to their friends and relatives that you personally gave them the recipe."

"You really are crazy," said the President.

"Those exercise shows, too," said Schulz. "Just about everyone in the country is on some sort of diet. You can talk about the diet you're on . . ."

"I'm not on a diet," said the President.

"You will be," said Schulz.

"You want me to go on shows about eating and then you want me to go on shows about dieting and exercise?" asked the President. "Won't someone point out the inconsistency?"

"I want you to cover all the bases," said Schulz. "Hey, we're going to reach all the voters and show them 'regular guy' Jack Newell who just happens to be President of the United States."

"You forgot the kiddie shows, Bill," said the President.

Once again Schulz simply ignored the sarcasm. "The talk shows, too. We end the campaign by hitting the talk shows."

"Not the crazy ones," said the President. "I'm not going on *Geraldo*. I won't do it. Sorry. But I've got to draw the line somewhere."

"No, no," said Schulz. "The good ones. *The Tonight Show*. I can see it now, you and Jay Leno. Fantastic. He's funny as hell. And after you do the show I'll bet he quits doing jokes about you. Or at least tones them down."

"You planning to have me sing and dance and play the guitar, or just talk?" asked the President.

"*Late Night with David Letterman* and *Arsenio Hall* would be good, too," said Schulz. "They reach the younger audience. Yeah, end with those shows. Talk about your experiences on the other shows. Say how much fun it was. No issues. None of that crap. Talk about how exciting it was for you to meet so many famous personalities like Vanna. Say that you're thinking about writing an article about being on all these great shows. *TV Guide* will jump at it. So will *People* magazine. Millions of people read that stuff. We'll load the articles with photos of you with Vanna and Jay and Dave and Arsenio and Phil and Oprah. People will love it. Absolutely love it. And do you know what is so fantastic about all this?"

"Do tell me," said the President.

"Stupp won't be able to do a damned thing to compete with the incredible p.r. you'll be getting. Poor son-of-a-bitch will have to go out and commit a crime or something to get back into the news."

"What about *Nightline* or *Sixty Minutes* or something like that?" asked the President.

"Don't be ridiculous," said Schulz. "The whole idea is to show you out of the context of your presidential responsibilities. To project you as a person the voters can identify with and root for. Haven't you been listening to me?"

"Why is it being foolish to mention programs that are watched by people who are interested in issues?" asked the President.

"You keep trying to jerk my chain," said Schulz. "You want to ask a good question? Ask why they call it *Sixty Minutes*. Why don't they call it *One Hour*?"

"I don't know," said the President. "Why don't they call it *One Hour*?

"How the hell should I know?" said Schulz.

"What I'd like to know," said the President, "is if this is such a great idea, why is it that no other President of the United States has ever done it? I'm sure they all had their reasons for not doing anything like this."

"They all had the same reason," said Schulz.

"And what is that?" asked the President.

"They didn't think of it," said Bill Schulz.

# Nine

As Bill Schulz was leaving the Oval Office and the President was starting to walk back to his desk, the President suddenly stopped in his tracks and turned and called Schulz back.

"Hold on a minute, Bill, we forgot the best part."

"What?" asked Schulz.

"You mentioned the other day that you would come up with some ideas about getting rid of Bates."

"I don't think that's quite what I said," answered Schulz.

"You did," said the President. "You said something to the effect that any really good strategy should also provide for getting rid of 'The Jerk.' I remember your saying that."

"It's not the sort of thing we can discuss on the run like this," said Schulz.

"I want to talk about it," said the President. "Come on back. Let's take an extra ten minutes to talk about it. I'm already running a little behind today. Another ten minutes won't matter much."

Bill Schulz reluctantly walked back into the Oval Office and sat down again on one of the sofas near the fireplace.

"How do we do it?" asked the President. "How do we get rid of him?"

"I wasn't being serious," said Schulz. "It was just something that came out. It's not like I really meant it. It's just that what you had said the other day made this crazy idea pop into my mind."

The President looked puzzled. "Something I said? What do you mean? I don't follow you."

"Look, I'm holding you up," said Schulz. "Maybe we should talk about this some other time."

"Just wait a minute," said the President. "Wait just a minute. Something is very strange here. You just characterized one of your own ideas as 'crazy'—this idea that you are so reluctant to let me in on. Now that's weird. Something's strange here. I've heard one hell of a lot of ideas out of you that I've thought were pretty crazy. You're not going to get away with thinking up one that even you think is nutty and then not tell me what it is. No way. This is something I want to hear."

"Forget it," said Schulz. "It's not what you think. I don't have any clever plan for getting rid of Bates. Really."

"Bull," said the President. "You're not leaving until I discover what you think is a truly nutty idea. This has got to be something really mad." The President laughed. Bill Schulz didn't.

"Please," said Schulz. "I shouldn't have said anything. I really shouldn't have said anything."

"Well, you did," said the President. "Spit it out."

"You're not going to like it," said Schulz, "and I don't blame you. Besides, it's embarrassing."

"Let me decide that," said the President. "Come on. Let's hear it."

"I told you," said Schulz. "There's no clever idea. I just think you should dump Bates. That's all."

"You can't bullshit me, Bill," said the President. "And you can't duck out of it. What was it that I said that made you bring up the idea of bumping Bates from the ticket? You said it was something I said. What? What the hell did I say? Tell me, dammit."

"It was, well, ah, all that business about 'somehow, some-way, no matter what it takes,' you were going to, well, you know . . ."

"Are you saying what I think you're saying?" asked the President.

"Yeah, dammit, I am," said Schulz. "I'm sorry. For a mo-ment I had this silly daydream about, well, you know, run-ning with you myself. I know it's wacky to think such a thing. It's ridiculous. I'm sorry. OK? Now will you get off my back. You're embarrassing me. You're making me feel like an idiot."

"Bill, I never imagined such a thing," said the President.

"I said I'm sorry," said Schulz. "Come on. Knock it off."

"Hey, don't be embarrassed," said the President. "There's no need for you to feel ill at ease. You're absolutely right. We should dump Bates. I can't stand the son-of-a-bitch and it would be a disaster for the country if he ever, God forbid, actually became President. We can't have him a heartbeat away. We just can't permit that. We can excuse our making the mistake of having picked him. But you're right, we can't excuse not correcting the mistake."

"I never said that," said Schulz.

"It's what you were thinking," said the President. "And you were right to think that."

"You dump him and the media will be all over you and so will half the Party," said Schulz.

"We'll ease him out," said the President. "Maybe convince him that for his own political future he'd be better off giving up the Vice Presidential nomination this time so he could better position himself for a run four years from now. Try to convince him that we're a lost cause and it can only hurt him if he's identified with it in any way."

"He might be dumb enough to buy that," said Schulz, "but if he didn't, well, trying to force him off the ticket would be a real problem, no matter how successful our 'regular guy' p.r. campaign goes for you."

"The hard, cold, difficult truth," said the President, "is that we need a new Vice Presidential candidate."

"Easier said than done," said Schulz.

"And your recommendation?" asked the President.

"Ah, come on," said Schulz. "Knock it off. I should have kept my big mouth shut. I wish the hell I didn't always tell you exactly what I think about everything. You're never going to let me live this down, are you?"

"Bill, there's nothing wrong with being ambitious," said the President. "It's no more ridiculous to talk about your running for Vice President today than it was four years ago to talk about my running for President. Not a bit more far-fetched."

"We both know *that* was incredibly far-fetched," said Schulz, breaking into a big grin. "Come on, let's change the subject."

"Hey, I'm not ribbing you," said the President. "I'm not being sarcastic. I mean it. I really do. There's nothing wrong with your thinking such an idea. And there sure as hell is nothing wrong with your sharing your thoughts with your friend. I am surprised. I'll admit that. I never would have guessed it. I can't think of anything you have ever said or done that would lead me to believe that this was an ambition of yours. So don't be surprised if I sound surprised."

"I just got carried away for a moment," said Schulz. "I just got caught up in a euphoric feeling, what with our patching things back together and all."

The truth, of course, was that the idea of being Jack Newell's running mate was not just a spur of the moment day-dream. It was a day-dream that had popped into Bill Schulz's head long ago. And it had never left. But he didn't want to admit that to Jack Newell.

"Let's discuss it," said the President. "Not right now, of course. But let's discuss it. Let's not rule anything out. Hell, I've made some pretty unusual commitments to you recently which I still find absolutely amazing that I ever went along with . . ."

"What commitments?" interrupted Schulz.

"You know," said the President. "Doing all these 'regular guy' goofy stunts that you keep coming up with."

"And going on *Wheel of Fortune* and all those other shows," said Schulz.

"Well . . ." said the President.

"Well, what?" asked Schulz.

"I want to ponder that a little more," said the President.

"Don't tell me you're getting chicken?" said Schulz.

The President stood up, signalling that the meeting was over. "Look," he said, "I've decided to follow this 'regular guy' strategy of yours and I've decided to dump Bates."

"Sure you will," said Schulz.

"Yeah, I mean it," said the President. "I'm dumping 'The Jerk.' I don't give a shit what anybody thinks."

"Come on," said Schulz. "Quit the teasing."

"I mean it," said the President. "Now those are two pretty damned serious political decisions I've made in the past few weeks. Give me a day and I'll give you my decision on whether or not I am also willing to go so far as to attempt to entertain the American people by making a fool of myself on *Wheel of Fortune* and those other TV shows. Fair enough?"

The President walked over to Bill Schulz and put his hand on Schulz's shoulder. "Bill, about this Vice President thing. Let's talk. You're absolutely right, I do owe a lot to you. Hell, I owe the Presidency to you. And I do have some atoning to do. Shit, I have a lot of atoning to do. If I could hand you the Vice Presidency, I probably should do it. You're the only person I really owe anything to politically. But everything is happening so fast. I need to think. We have to weigh everything. We need to look at the whole picture. Then we need to talk again. Real soon."

"Sure," said Schulz.

"I mean that, Bill," said the President. "I am not saying 'no.' And I'm not ducking it."

"What *are* you saying, Jack?" asked Schulz.

"I'm saying that we need to really think this through," said the President. "I'd like to do it. Believe me, I'd like to do it. One thing is damned certain: We're dumping Bates. No matter what, I can't have it on my conscience that I permitted him to remain a heartbeat away from the Presidency. As far as putting you on the ticket, hell, it just might not change much. People vote for President, not Vice President, anyhow." He caught himself. "I didn't mean . . ."

"You're really serious, aren't you?" asked Schulz.

"I'm always serious," said the President. "I thought you said that's the problem with me."

Bill Schulz smiled. The President walked Schulz to the door. "I'm running late for a meeting with the National Security Council on that Latin American problem," he said, as they stood at the door. "At noon I have to give that National Press Club speech on the economy. Then I have to go up to Walter Reed for my annual physical. I've postponed it three times before and they're screaming that it's been nearly a year-and-a-half since my last so-called annual physical. Then this evening I've got this state dinner for the Prime Minister of Australia."

"Then you'd better get back to work," said Schulz.

"I want to pick up on our conversation right where we left off just as soon as I can," said the President.

"Anytime you want," said Schulz.

"I want to do it today," said the President. "Let's do this. Look, you and Lynne are coming to the state dinner this evening. As quickly as I can ditch the guests, how about you send Lynne home and then you and I will have a quiet cocktail together and discuss all this?" Schulz said that was fine with him.

As Bill Schulz left the White House and headed to his car, he thought about how much had changed in the past few weeks. It was just like the good ole days once again. It was exciting. Invigorating. Fun. And—holy shit!—the President of the United States wants to sit down with him this evening in the White House for yet another very private discussion. And among the topics of conversation will be the possibility of William Schulz's becoming the candidate for Vice President of the United States.

Which, of course, could lead to . . .

"Wow!" Bill Schulz said aloud.

No one heard him.

# Ten

If there is one thing that the nine justices of the United States Supreme Court have in common it is that each of them likes to follow precedent when at all possible. But probably not one of the nine could explain why or when the justices had come up with the only precedent that they all agreed on.

They just did it. It was habit. During the January to May season during which they normally decide their major cases, on Tuesdays, the usual day for handing down opinions, along about seven-thirty in the evening each of the nine justices would head over to Connecticut Avenue. There at their favorite restaurant—*Joe & Mo's*—they would sit down together, just the nine of them, and enjoy fine drinks and a superb dinner accompanied with some first-class wine. And over drinks and dinner this gang of nine also savored some very lively, very frank conversation.

It was like a club. A secret club. The understanding was that anything they discussed with one another at *Joe & Mo's* was never to be repeated to anyone else. Not to their spouses. Not to their best friends. Not to any clerks of the Court. And, of course, not to any journalists.

Nor was anything that was said there, no matter how dumb or outrageous, ever to be thrown up to one another in any conversation that took place anywhere else.

Mo Sussman always greeted each of them individually. That was part of the ritual. And in the course of the evening each justice usually managed to check out the walls to make sure that his or her photo autographed to Mo, or his or her book autographed to Mo, still occupied a portion of one of the more prominent walls of the restaurant.

Although none of them ever mentioned it, it bothered them a great deal that almost every time they were there some of the patrons in the restaurant were whispering and pointing out the celebrities present—and the whispering and the pointing was never about any of them. Never.

Not one of them ever seemed to notice, at least not one of them ever mentioned noticing it, but there was one habit common to each of them. In almost all of their most memorable discussions at these *Joe & Mo's* sessions an awful lot of their sentences began with "If I were President" or "If I were running Congress" or some similar phrase.

The sort of phrase that a strict constructionist would surely interpret as an incontrovertible sign that, deep down, these nine individuals who had been selected by one elected official and blessed by a majority vote of other elected officials really *did* want to run both other branches of the federal government, not just their own much smaller operation.

They talked about the Vice President a great deal.

"Why does everyone always call him 'The Jerk'?" asked Justice Lonny Dolin, the court's lone female justice.

"Well, it isn't because he starred in the Steve Martin movie of that name," said Justice Wayne DeHond. "And it isn't 'everyone.' The public seems to think he's OK. It's only those who truly know him who seem to understand."

"They call him 'The Jerk' for the same reason they call red red and blue blue," said Justice John Considine. "Because it's the correct label; it's what he is."

It was at *Joe & Mo's* that the nine of them made their pact.

These nine individuals who so frequently split five to four, these nine individuals who so seldom agreed on any issue at greater than a six to three ratio, over dinner that night these nine individuals all enthusiastically agreed on one thing. Republican or Democrat, conservative or liberal, legal scholar or former politician, each justice agreed with equal fervor on one matter that all of them felt to be of crucial importance to the country.

Right there at *Joe & Mo's* that night the nine justices of the Supreme Court vowed to one another that they would do anything they could think of to thwart the presidential ambitions of "The Jerk." Anything.

They just about took a blood oath on it.

"But what can we do?" they kept asking one another.

And finally the Chief Justice of the United States, Richard E. Stowe, said: "We'll think of something."

They didn't resolve anything over dinner and drinks that evening. But they all left *Joe & Mo's* feeling pretty good about their little conspiracy to band together and engage in some good old-fashioned judicial activism. And they all looked forward to subsequent discussions about this topic at their future *Joe & Mo's* sessions.

For they all knew that, when pressed, the Supreme Court can be incredibly imaginative.

# Eleven

B ill Schulz's secretary buzzed his intercom. "It's the President calling," she announced.

The President opened the conversation by asking Schulz if he had reminded Lynne about the state dinner for the Prime Minister of Australia that evening. He had. And had he mentioned to her that the President wanted him to remain afterwards for a little private chat? He had.

"Well, look, Bill," said the President, "I've been thinking. It's difficult to break away from a state dinner for a private chat . . ."

"I understand," Schulz interrupted. "We can do it some other time."

"No, no," said the President. "What I was thinking is this: It's easier to get away if you're going somewhere. Well, today's Friday. What I'll do is spend the weekend at Camp David. That way, I can just walk out to the South Lawn when the formalities are finished and get in the chopper and not have to linger around."

"Have a nice weekend," said Schulz.

"No, no, you've got the wrong idea," said the President. "The reason I'm calling is that I'd like you to pack some clothes and bring them with you when you come to dinner this evening. Just have your driver give your suitcase to one of the Secret Service guys near the helicopter. Sometime after dinner one of the agents will come over to your table and take you out and put you in the chopper. Plan on being up at Camp David tonight and tomorrow night, too, if that's okay with you. We'll come back probably mid-Sunday afternoon."

"Sure. Sounds great," said Schulz. "I look forward to it."

"I find I can think better up there," said the President, "and you and I are going to be doing some heavy thinking this weekend."

"Anyone else going to be joining us?" asked Schulz.

"Bill, there are no other heavy thinkers in Washington," joked the President. "See you this evening."

Schulz called his wife and asked if she could set out some clothes for him to take to Camp David for the weekend. He had called her a couple hours earlier to tell her all the details about his latest meeting with the President and to tell her that he would be staying on at the White House for yet another private chat with the President.

"Camp David!" said Lynne Schulz. "Now he's taking you to Camp David? Great!"

Schulz told his wife what he needed packed for his Camp David weekend and asked her what she planned to wear that night. After he hung up the telephone, he sat back and stared at his office for a couple of minutes. It was a splendid office. Palatial by most standards. But it wasn't the place he wanted to be. True, lots of people would kill to have the President name them Director of the United States Information Agency. Especially people in the advertising/public relations business. It's the sort of job that provides prestige for today and the promise of opening up all sorts of interesting future opportunities.

But Bill Schulz's dreams were larger than that. Much larger. And for the first time—and to his utter amazement—they had been spoken aloud to another person. All these years and he had never even hinted it to his own wife. He still couldn't believe he had actually said it to the President.

Actually said that he wanted to be Vice President. Which, of course, is really just a different way some people have of saying that they want to be President.

As he and Lynne pulled into the White House for the state dinner for the Prime Minister of Australia that evening, Bill Schulz was in high spirits as he reminded his driver about getting his suitcase to one of the Secret Service agents near the helicopter.

His driver remarked that he had spent quite a bit of time at the White House this day and asked if he expected to be spending so much time there from now on.

"Arnaldo," said Schulz, "I expect to be spending a great deal of time at the White House from here on in. A great deal of time. Someday I may even have it painted a different color."

# Twelve

Camp David is only 75 miles from the White House, just a half-hour hop in *Marine One*, the Presidential helicopter, but it seems a million miles from the pressures that always permeate the White House.

The President loved to come here. Before he was President, he could never understand why Eisenhower and those who followed him in office were always running off to this little mountain retreat in Maryland. Now he understood. There was indeed something about the serenity of the place that seemed to help a President's mind do a better job of placing things in perspective.

The President excused the servants for the evening and headed straight to the bar. "Bombay martini on the rocks with two olives, right?"

"Right," said Schulz.

"Bill," said the President, as he handed Schulz his drink, "I have some good news and some bad news. Sit down. We need to talk."

"Don't tell me those doctors at Walter Reed prescribed some new jokes for you," said Schulz.

"Wish they had," said the President. "Wish they had. No, I'm afraid this is no joke. I suppose I should mention the good news first. I thought about our conversation this morning very seriously after you left. Very seriously. And then I made a decision. I decided I really would love to have you run for Vice President with me . . ."

"Are you serious?" asked Bill Schulz.

"Hold on, my friend," said the President. "It doesn't matter. Because the bad news is that I can't ask you. I am a sick man. A very sick man. I cannot run for re-election."

Bill Schulz felt a pain shoot through his entire body. "Oh, my God!"

The President sat down in the chair across from him. Neither man spoke. Both were pale. Finally the President spoke. He explained that he had not been feeling well for quite some time, that during the day he would have moments when suddenly he felt very weak and during the night he sometimes woke up with an excruciating pain in his side followed by a frightful shortness of breath.

He said he knew that he should have gone to the doctor when it first started happening, but, well, he had never had any problems with his health. Never. Except, of course, for an occasional cold, and he had those far less often than nearly anyone else he knew. So he had just kept hoping that this problem would pass in due time.

"I'm glad Nancy's not here to see this," said the President. His wife had died a few weeks after he had been elected President. He said that if his wife had still been alive she would have made him tell the doctors about it, but, well, with her gone he just didn't care that much about taking care of himself. The only reason he had even bothered to go to Walter Reed for the check-up, he said, was because it looked odd that he had kept postponing it.

As delicately as he could, Bill Schulz tried to ask the President just exactly what was wrong with him and exactly how serious it was.

"There's a big long medical term for what I've got," said the President. "They've even named it after some foreign guy, so you know it has to be a real good one, huh?"

"How serious?" asked Schulz.

"Damned serious," said the President. "It changes every-thing. Everything."

"Why didn't they keep you in the hospital?" asked Schulz.

"They would have preferred that," said the President.

"Then how come you're not there?" asked Schulz.

"You can figure out why," said the President. "Look, you know what would have happened if I had stayed in the hospital. It'd be a big news story."

"Well, sure," said Schulz.

"I need some time to think it through," said the President. "Believe me, it is much wiser right now for me to just sit here and relax and have a quiet cocktail and talk things through with you and with no one else around than it would be to have me laying in some damn hospital bed with the news media screaming outside the doors. Right?"

"Did the doctors say that you should go into the hospital right away?" asked Schulz.

"They said they preferred that I did," said the President. "But they didn't say I had to."

Schulz brightened up a bit. "Then maybe it's really not that bad."

"It's that bad," said the President. "Real bad. I promised them I wouldn't exert myself. They made me promise. They said that I face a serious risk of dropping dead . . . "

"Good God!" said Bill Schulz.

"Unless pretty damn soon I get away for a complete rest for a few weeks," continued the President. "A complete rest. Not a working vacation. A real vacation. They said I should get away to some nice tranquil sunny spot and just totally relax. Lay on the beach and maybe do some snorkeling. I told them about how you always rave about doing that in Fiji. Know what they said? They said Fiji would be perfect. One of the doctors had been there and he raved about the place. I should go there just as soon as I can. That's what they said. Can you believe that?"

"Fiji?" said Schulz. "How the hell can you get away for a three week vacation in Fiji? You're President of the United States, Jack. You can't just pack up and go off on vacation."

"I told them that, Bill," said the President. "I reminded them that the President of the United States doesn't just take a vacation, a real genuine vacation, like he's some run-of-the-mill slob or something."

"What'd they say to that?" asked Schulz.

"They said that's what we have a Vice President for—to step in and handle things when the President is unable to perform his duties. And—they're clever, they think of every-thing—one of the doctors even pulled out these old news-magazine articles to show me how Eisenhower's popularity in the polls increased significantly while he was recovering from his heart attack. Another doctor remarked that Ike did damn well at re-election time despite his having had to spend so much time recuperating."

"Holy shit!" said Bill Schulz so suddenly and unexpect-edly that it startled the President.

"What is it?" asked the President.

" 'The Jerk'," said Schulz. "That jerk Bernie Bates is going to preside over the government of the United States!"

"That's exactly what kept going through my mind," said the President. "Hell, I didn't feel all that godawful sick until this image of Bates in the Oval Office kept going through my mind."

"This is horrible," said Schulz.

"I mean, how the hell can I go off and lounge around some beach and leave the reins of government in his hands?" said the President. "It's frightening, that's what it is. And it's depressing. All our great plans down the drain. Just when I was finally really believing that I could be re-elected and dump Bates and have you right there at my side like you deserve to be. Shit!"

"Have you told anyone about this?" asked Schulz.

"Just you," said the President.

"What about the doctors?" asked Schulz.

"Bill, they're the ones who told me," said the President.

Schulz was surprised that the President would joke around at a time like this. "Let me finish," said Schulz. "What about the doctors? Have they told anyone?"

"Not really," said the President.

"Will they be telling anyone?" asked Schulz.

"Not right away," said the President. "Eventually, of course. But not right away."

"Don't they have to issue some sort of medical statement on you?" asked Schulz. "After all, it was in the papers, naturally, that your schedule today included a medical checkup at Walter Reed."

"One of the things that still seems to be sacred in the world, even in Washington, D.C., is doctor-patient confidentiality," said the President. "Yes, Bill, the doctors have issued a statement. I helped them write it. What it says is that they have examined me thoroughly and I am every bit as fit as I have been for the past year and a half."

"Well, that's not true," said Schulz.

"Yes, it is," said the President. "They estimate that I've had this for a year and a half now."

"Wait a minute!" said Schulz. "That medical statement makes it sound like you have no problems."

"Only to those who don't know that for the past year and a half I've been afflicted with something very serious," said the President.

Schulz was surprised that the most honest politician in America was clearly determined to deceive the American people about such a startling development.

"Isn't it against the law to falsify a medical report on the President of the United States?" asked Schulz.

"I would imagine it's against the law to falsify any medical report," said the President. "But then only one of us went to law school and it wasn't me."

"What the hell are you up to?" asked Schulz.

"Bill, we're not saying I'm well," said the President. "We're saying that I'm as well as I've been during the period when I haven't been well."

"I can't believe the doctors would let you get away with this," said Schulz.

"They are military doctors and I am the Commander-in-Chief," said the President. "Now I didn't order them to lie. I just sort of helped them find a more creative way of telling the truth."

"So you're not expecting anything to be in the news?" asked Schulz.

"No," said the President. "The press briefing was held late this afternoon and what I caught on the radio news was a couple seconds report mentioning that I had been at the hospital for a brief routine check and I was —how did they put it?—"as fit as he has been in a long time."

Schulz suddenly remembered hearing that on the radio. "Hey, that's right. I heard the news. It didn't even register with me. You pulled it off. Holy shit! You fooled everyone."

"I've bought some time," said the President. "Some time to think before I have to face up to it, that's all. You can't fool Mother Nature."

"What should we do now?" asked Schulz.

"We should get some sleep now," said the President. "It's already after midnight. I should have known I couldn't slip away early. I'd kinda like to sleep on things and then get a fresh start in the morning. It's been quite a day."

*"It sure as shit has been quite a day,"* Bill Schulz thought to himself. *"It sure as shit has."*

# Thirteen

The President had been awake and sitting in the den for nearly an hour, reading his morning newspapers and his special White House briefing papers and having his morning coffee and eating a danish, while Bill Schulz finished showering and shaving.

He was sipping his second cup of coffee when Schulz walked in the room. "Where'd you get that coffee?" asked Schulz.

"Out in the kitchen," said the President. "Help yourself. I sent the servants off."

"What the hell did you do that for?" said Schulz. "I like being waited on."

"We don't want anyone overhearing our conversation," said the President. "Bring the coffee pot in here, will you? I forgot to do that. After you have your coffee and grab a bite I want us to start working on my resignation speech."

"Resignation speech?" asked Schulz.

"Yeah, what the hell did you expect to do this morning?" said the President. "Go snorkeling?"

Schulz brought the coffee pot from the kitchen and walked over to Jack Newell and poured a refill into the President's cup. Then he poured himself a cup and set the coffee pot on the hot plate that was on the coffee table. He sat down across from the President. He reached across the coffee table and picked up a danish from a dish heaped high with breakfast bakery items. He started speaking with his mouth still half full. "You say it like you like the idea. Like you're relieved."

"Resignation is the only thing I can do," said the President. "It's in the best interest of the country."

"You sound like Nixon," said Schulz.

"Thanks a lot," said the President.

"He resigned," said Schulz. "That how you want history to remember you? You and Nixon—only two Presidents ever to resign?"

"I think people will remember that the circumstances were different," said the President.

The two men sat silently for a few moments drinking coffee and eating danish and breakfast rolls. Schulz glanced quickly through *The Washington Post, The Washington Times, The Wall Street Journal* and *The New York Times*, all of which the President had already read cover to cover.

It was Schulz who broke the silence. "You can't do it, Jack. I already know what you should say. And what you should say is: Nothing! Not a damn thing."

"Oh, sure," said the President, sarcastically.

"Seriously," said Schulz. "I was awake half the night thinking about it. You can't resign. You can't let 'The Jerk' become President of the United States."

"It's not what I would have chosen," said the President. "But I don't have much choice, do I?"

"Of course you do," said Schulz. "You're the damned President. You can do what you want. You can hang in there. You have to."

"Were you listening when we talked last night," said the President. "There's no choice. Either I walk away or they carry me away. It's that simple."

Schulz shook his head vigorously. "No, no. It's not that simple."

"Bill, this is a very simple straightforward matter of life or death. My life. My death. So come on. Let's think about how we should put it to the American people."

"You'll be putting it to the American people, all right, if you resign," said Schulz.

"Come on," said the President. "Let's get drafting a statement."

"You don't want to resign," said Schulz. "And you can't resign. Just get that out of your head and let's get serious."

"I *do* want to resign," said the President. "I have to."

"That's nice and convenient, isn't it?" said Schulz.

The President was startled. "What?"

"It lets you off the hook, doesn't it?" said Schulz. "No more fear of defeat. No tough race to worry about. Convenient. Very convenient."

The President got up from his chair and started to walk over to the coffee pot. After he poured himself a half cup of coffee, he turned to Schulz: "I can't believe you said that, Bill. I can't believe anyone would say such a thing to a dying man."

"Maybe you can't believe I'd say it," said Schulz, "but you do believe it's the truth, don't you?"

"Yeah, you bastard, I suppose I do feel some sense of relief," said the President.

"You cannot let 'The Jerk' become President," said Schulz. "You can't do such a thing to the country. Besides, resign and you know what's going to happen to you? You'll end up as a 'Trivial Pursuit' question!"

"A 'Trivial Pursuit' question?" said the President. "What the hell is that supposed to mean?"

"You know," said Schulz, "'What other President besides Nixon resigned?' That what you want?"

"My, my, don't we have a high regard for the accomplishments of the Newell Administration," said the President.

"You know what I mean," said Schulz, "It'll dwarf everything else."

"Let's get on with the resignation," said the President.

"Nixon!"

The President smiled. "Bill, I'd bet that if you had been around at the time that Nixon was about to resign and they had come to you for advice you would have recommended against his resigning."

"I would not have recommended resignation," said Schulz.

"You really think Nixon should have tried to hang in there?" asked the President in a tone of voice that showed he was genuinely surprised at Schulz's comment.

"I didn't say that," said Schulz.

"Then you think he should have been impeached?" asked the President.

"I didn't say that either," said Schulz.

"Wait a minute," said the President. "Wait just a minute. You're saying that you wouldn't have recommended resignation. You're saying that you wouldn't have recommended his staying in office. You're saying that you wouldn't have recommended impeachment. Bill, there is nothing left that you could have recommended."

"Sure there is," said Schulz.

"What?" asked the President.

"Crucifixion," said Schulz.

"I knew I shouldn't have asked," said the President.

"Just think about it a moment," said Schulz. "Crucifixion would have been the perfect compromise. A graceful face-saving way out for everyone."

The President shook his head and grinned just a bit.

"There's a nice historical connotation to it," Schulz went on. "Hell, the guy did see himself as a martyr. I'd bet his most diehard defenders would have been sort of proud to see a crucifixion held in his honor."

"You're the one who's sick," said the President.

"Ah, but what would his enemies have gotten out of it, you wonder," said Schulz. "The satisfaction of seeing him nailed to the cross. Which is what they always wanted."

The President made his usual gesture of shaking his head and rolling his eyes.

"It would have been a great ceremony," Schulz went on. "Lots of symbolism. Think of it. Instead of Calvary Hill we'd have Capitol Hill. He'd walk from the White House down Pennsylvania Avenue to Capitol Hill. The inaugural route in reverse—how's that for symbolism? Only one flaw in the whole plan."

The President remarked that he knew he really shouldn't ask what the flaw was, but he would anyhow.

"The thieves," said Schulz. "Remember? There were two thieves. Hell, with Nixon we could have covered Capitol Hill with thieves. As far as the eye could see—rows and rows of thieves. Of course, there'd be even more —ten times as many—if it were Lyndon Johnson."

"That's the flaw, huh?" said the President.

"The flaw," said Schulz, "is that there's supposed to be a good thief, remember? There wasn't a good thief among that whole gang."

"Could you be serious for a minute?" said the President.

"I can be dead serious, if that's what you'd really prefer," said Schulz. "I was just trying to lighten things up."

"I think I'll be dead before you're ever serious," said the President. "Let me get this straight. You're saying, you're thinking, that I should ignore what the doctors told me."

"No," said Schulz. "Not at all. You're the one who hasn't been listening carefully. That's not at all what I think. Quite the opposite. I think you should do exactly what the doctors told you. Exactly. Like I said, you're the one who hasn't been listening very carefully. You didn't hear what I've been saying. And apparently you didn't hear what the doctors told you either."

"What?" said the President. "You're not making sense."

"What did the doctors tell you?" asked Schulz.

"You know what the hell they told me," said the President.

"They did *not* tell you to resign, did they?" said Schulz. "No, they did *not*. What they told you is to get away and totally relax for a few weeks. That's what they told you that you had to do. Not resign."

"You make it sound like I've had a nervous breakdown or something," said the President. "I'm sick, Bill. Not tired or exhausted. I have this peculiar illness. Now I have to—the sooner the better—get away for perhaps three weeks of total rest. But that doesn't mean that once I've done that I'm OK. No, it means that if I don't do that I'll probably drop dead. The resting isn't a cure. It just helps me stay alive longer."

"I understand all that," said Schulz.

"Well I'm afraid I don't understand what you're driving at," said the President.

"I'm thinking about 'The Jerk,'" said Schulz. "I'm thinking about the prospect of Bates' becoming President. There has to be a way to stop it."

"You don't think I've thought of that?" asked the President. "Believe me, I've thought it through. Resigning is the best way to deal with the Bates problem."

"That doesn't make a lick of sense," said Schulz. "You resign and what happens? 'The Jerk' becomes President. Simple."

"No, Bill, it's not so damn simple," said the President. "Not if you bother to think it through. If I die in office, he becomes President. If I resign, he becomes President. On the surface, aside from my getting a bit nicer state funeral, there doesn't appear to be any great difference. But there really is a great difference. One hell of a great difference. If I die in office, there is a stronger danger—you know it—that the country would rally behind Bates with all that sentimental crap about giving the new President time to prove himself. Under such circumstances, the dumb voters are likely to elect him this Fall. That means the country has 'The Jerk' in the Oval Office for roughly four and a half years. But if I resign rather than die in office, there is much less of a sympathy factor—much less! My guess is that under those circumstances Stupp would win in November and 'The Jerk' would be President for less than half a year, not four and a half years."

"Oh, great!" said Schulz, sarcastically. "That way the country would get both 'The Jerk' and the airhead actor!"

"It's the best way to insure that we minimize Bates' time

as President," said the President. "It's a terrible option, I'll admit, but it's the only real option we have."

"No, it's not," said Schulz. "It's the easiest option, but it's not the only option."

"And what you suggest is that I ignore the doctors," said the President.

"No, I didn't say that you ignore them," said Schulz. "I told you I think you should do what they said. That is . . ."

The President interrupted. "And you think I should conceal my health problems from the public?"

"Yes," said Schulz. "I do think that. I think that because I think it is in the national interest."

"To hell with the public's right to know? Isn't that what you're really saying?" asked the President.

Schulz argued that "the public's right to know" is very often little more than a leveling phrase employed by status-minded journalists, a shockingly high percentage of whom, in his view, cared very little about the public or its right to know while they cared very much about the ego gratification that comes from having convinced a large share of the public that the media has entitlement rights to anything that the President thinks or does and that they, more so than the voting public, are the ones who really should be grading the performance of the President and other public officials.

"There is nothing wrong with keeping your thoughts and the facts about your health to yourself," said Schulz, "if that's what it takes to spare the country from 'The Jerk.'"

"I wish it could be done," said the President. "I really do."

"You do have to do what the doctors told you," said Schulz. "You have got to get away for a complete rest for a few weeks . . ."

"Bill, give up," said the President. "Face the facts. The President of the United States cannot just drop out of the picture for a few weeks. You can't fool the whole damn country."

Schulz argued that the days when the American public required the image of the President's carrying the burden of the world on his shoulders twenty-four hours a day, every day of the month, every month of the year, had passed. He reminded Jack Newell about Ike's frequent golf trips and Ronald Reagan's pretty much closing down the White House and going off to his California ranch for a few weeks every summer and George Bush's hunting and fishing forays even during a period while he was putting together the highly successful Gulf War and again while the former Soviet Union was going through its August 1991 revolution.

The President countered that while his predecessors did indeed get away from it all they did so in a way that involved taking it all right along with them, too. He said that the doctors said he needed to *truly* get away to relax and that he needed to do so just as soon as possible. He emphasized that the strain of all his key aides "vacationing" with him and the strain of the nation's news media accompanying him and reporting every aspect of his "vacation" just wouldn't do. He said that he had to take a real vacation—"just like everybody else does"—and that was simply impossible for a sitting President to do.

"Suppose we could come up with a way for you to get a real vacation?" asked Schulz. "Suppose you could have a genuine vacation, as you put it, 'just like everyone else' . . ."

"Can't be done," interrupted the President.

"And suppose," continued Schulz, "that the media had something else to cover that appealed to them so much that they hardly bothered you at all?"

"Could never happen," said the President.

"But just suppose there was a way?" asked Schulz. "Under those circumstances, would you hang in there and spare the country from being subjected to 'The Jerk' as President?"

"Yeah, sure," said the President. "But that's impossible, and you know it."

"OK," said Bill Schulz, "then it's all set. You'll go on that real, genuine get-away-from-it-all vacation and get all the rest you need and then when the campaign moves into higher gear I'll do all the real work and we'll keep a tight lid on any strain on you. I'll see to that."

The President smiled and shook his head. And then in his best sarcastic tone he said: "I'm going to go off on a royal holiday and then when I get back I'm not going to strain myself any while running for President of the United States. And we're going to win, too That's it, huh?"

"You got it," said Schulz. "Then you can step down later, if you have to."

"And let 'The Jerk' be President after all?" said the President. "Are you nuts?" He caught himself, but not before Bill Schulz jumped in.

"Hey, pay attention," said Schulz. "We're dumping Bates, remember?"

Suddenly the President began to feel a whole lot better. If he could hold out until after the election, and if he did win, and if he had dumped 'The Jerk,' and if he did what he and Bill Schulz were now *both* thinking, then—holy shit!—when he did die the Presidency would pass to his good friend Bill Schulz.

*"That would be fantastic!"* the President thought to himself. For awhile he felt euphoric. But soon his sense of realism returned.

"Bill, I don't like to pee on anybody's camp fire," said the President, "but I haven't heard you explain how the hell you think you can con the American public and the news media into going for an idea as ludicrous as having the President of the United States run off and drop out of everything for a genuine three-week get-away-from-it-all vacation."

"You *underestimate* the power of the Presidency," said Bill Schulz. "But that's not your big mistake."

"Oh?" said the President. "And what is my big mistake?"

"Your big mistake," said Bill Schulz, "is that you *overestimate* the media and the public."

# Fourteen

U p went the trial balloon.
     As he was leaving the White House the following
Friday afternoon for a weekend visit to his New Hampshire
farm ("the New England White House," as the news media
liked to call it), the President remembered to carry in his arms
the huge pile of papers that Bill Schulz had set out for him.

Television cameras closed in on him as he walked out the
diplomatic entrance of the White House and headed toward
the South Lawn where *Marine One*, the presidential helicopter, was awaiting him. The television reporters aimed their
microphones toward him and got ready to shout questions at
him. The print reporters stood next to them, clutching their
pads and pens, all set to shout.

The news media was always out in force. Just in case the
President of the United States might say or do something that
could be considered newsworthy. Of course, anything he said
or did was considered newsworthy. Which is why they were
always there.

Nearby, behind the ropes, was a crowd of mid- and lower-
level political appointees and their friends. The White House
had for years had a practice of passing out tickets to support-
ers and their curiosity-seeking friends admitting them to the

White House grounds to witness a Presidential departure. It always worked. A couple hundred of the faithful would always come by and wait patiently until the President emerged. Then they would wave and cheer at the President. It wasn't fake. They were, after all, the faithful and they were genuinely happy to be there. They liked the idea of being able to tell their friends that they had been to the White House and actually seen the President. Many of them took mostly out-of-focus photos to prove to themselves and their friends that they had gotten close. Their presence made a good background scene and good background noise for the evening news.

President Newell held up his pile of work and gestured with it toward the reporters. Then he looked straight into the lens of the television cameras. "I envy you people," he said.

"What was that, Mr. President?" asked CBS News.

"Could you speak up, Mr. President?" asked ABC News.

"Mr. President, could you turn this way so we can get a better shot of you?" asked NBC News.

"I said I envy you people," repeated the President.

"What do you mean, Mr. President?" asked Associated Press.

"I envy you people," he said for the third time. "When you get away from the job for a couple of days, you really get away from it."

The President stopped and paused just a second. He looked down at the pile of documents he was carrying in his arms. A contemplative look came over his face. Then he seemed to be trying to fake a smile. And then he resumed his pace, walking briskly toward the waiting helicopter without saying anything else.

"Now that was a profound interview," said The New York Times to The Washington Post.

"Was he trying to tell us something?" asked The Wall Street Journal of nobody in particular.

"Do you suppose there's some crisis he's keeping from us?" asked Newsweek.

"I don't think so," said United Press International. "He was in too good a mood."

"Maybe the guy is just relieved to be getting away from all the pressure for a nice quiet weekend," said Time.

USA Today scratched his head. The Washington Times was so engrossed in thinking about the exposé of yet another Congressional scandal which he alone among this army of reporters had uncovered that he didn't pay attention to this light exchange.

"I think Newell made a good point," said The Washington Post.

"What point?" asked a chorus of reporters.

"Hey, I'm not getting paid to write your stories for you," said The Washington Post. "Try to figure it out for yourselves. And if you can't, well, just pick up a copy of the world's greatest newspaper tomorrow morning." He smiled. *"There'll be a front-page photo of that poor bastard holding up all that damn work,"* he thought to himself. *"I guarantee it."*

Saturday morning most newspapers across the nation carried only a brief mention of the fact that the President was at his New Hampshire farm for the weekend and that he had taken with him a large load of work on undisclosed topics.

The Saturday edition of *The Washington Post*, however, carried a large front-page above-the-fold photo of the President standing outside the White House glancing down at a huge pile of work to be done. There was a contemplative look on his face.

Under the photo, the large type caption lead-in read: "VACATION—PRESIDENTIAL STYLE."

The text of the photo caption read:

"As he was leaving the White House yesterday for a brief weekend 'vacation' at his New Hampshire farm, President John Newell looked more like a man on his way to work than from it. Pausing briefly to talk with news media reporters, the President told the reporters that he 'envied' them. Why? Because, he pointed out, when they get a couple of days away from work, they really are able to get away from it and enjoy a genuine rest just like everyone else. Most reporters missed his point."

*"The Post didn't have to rub it in with that last line,"* both Associated Press and United Press International thought to themselves early Saturday morning, as they sat in their suburban Washington homes reading the *Washington Post.*

Associated Press called the office and dictated a photo caption. So did United Press International. On Sunday morning just about every newspaper of any size in the country had either an AP or UPI imitation of the photo-and-caption feature which had appeared in the Saturday morning *Washington Post.*

On Sunday morning's *Meet The Press,* the featured guest was the nationally-prominent junior Senator from Mississippi, Mike Massey, close personal friend of both the President and Bill Schulz.

The Senator, one of the most highly regarded members of Congress, remembered to remark that he had been talking with the President only moments before going on the air and that the President was "working terribly hard" during his "so-called weekend rest." He looked directly into the camera and said: "Isn't it a shame that the President of the United States never gets to enjoy a genuine vacation just like everyone else?"

On *This Week With David Brinkley,* Secretary of Commerce Tom Wilmot made a light comment about the tan he had just picked up during his week of golf in Bermuda. Then he remembered to pause dramatically for a couple of seconds and make one of those facial expressions that indicates that one has just thought of something new.

And then he looked up at the camera and said: "This might sound a bit funny, but I just happened to think of something that, well, something that I have never really thought about before. I feel really fresh and renewed because I was able to get away for awhile—completely away from the pressures of the job—and really get to relax. I'm going to be able to do a better job for the rest of the year because I was able to do that. Most of us take that for granted, don't we? For ourselves, at least, right? Well, I couldn't help noticing on the Friday night evening news, and then again in that picture in yesterday's *Washington Post* and this morning's *New York Times*, that my boss, The President, was carrying all that work with him on his way to what should be some rest but really isn't. Know what I mean?"

"Interesting," said David Brinkley.

"It just hit me," said Secretary Wilmot, "that, whether they did it intentionally or not, these reporters have made a strong point. Like I said, I never really thought about it myself until just now. Probably because the Friday evening news and the photo in *The Washington Post* yesterday and *The New York Times* this morning make the point so vividly."

"Which point do you mean?" asked George Will.

*"I like that,"* the Secretary of Commerce thought to himself. *"He doesn't say, 'What point?' No, that might make it look like there's something he hasn't thought of. So he says, 'Which point?' That makes it look like he not only knows what I'm thinking but also that there may be something that he's thought of that I haven't. Clever bastard."*

"That a real vacation is necessary in any job, especially in any stressful job," said Secretary Wilmot. "I just got back from vacation. I take a nice vacation every year. I bet you do, too."

"Sure," said George Will.

"And I bet you do, too, David," said the Secretary of Commerce.

"Of course," said David Brinkley.

"I don't," said Sam Donaldson.

"And it shows," joked Cokie Roberts.

"Just about everyone watching this program does," said Secretary Wilmot. "Sam's the exception."

"I'm not watching the program," said Sam Donaldson. "I'm in the program."

*"What an ass!"* Tom Wilmot thought to himself.

"Let him finish, Sam," said David Brinkley.

"I was just making the point that I can't be watching the program if I'm in the program," said Sam Donaldson.

*"Jerk!"* George Will thought to himself.

*"What an ass!"* Cokie Roberts thought to herself.

*"It's a wonder Reagan never punched him out,"* David Brinkley thought to himself.

The Secretary of Commerce continued: "There isn't a CEO of any large corporation in America—believe me, I know most of them—who doesn't take a genuine vacation every year. I mean, a real vacation. It doesn't hurt their businesses. In fact, most companies pretty much insist on it. They feel it's important to have their chief executive get completely away from the job for awhile. And not just for a few hours now and then. Not just for a couple of days at a time. A couple of weeks. Like I said, lots of companies now insist on that. Because they know that it helps make their CEO more efficient. I believe that. Most business leaders believe that."

"You're saying that most business leaders don't like to work," said Sam Donaldson. "Maybe that's our problem. Japanese businessmen sure like to work. And they don't get paid anywhere near as much as ours."

"Sam," said Tom Wilmot, *"you* need a vacation. You're not paying attention. You're not making sense. All I'm saying is that a genuine break now and then from the burdens of a very stressful job is almost universally recognized to be a sound idea. You are probably the only person in America, maybe the entire world, who would argue the opposite. And by the way, Sam, the Japanese don't believe in paying great sums of money to television reporters. Do you suppose that's the secret of their success?"

David Brinkley laughed. "The point I was making," continued the Secretary of Commerce, "is that it is a standard practice of our society, and it is a standard practice for very good reasons, that people once in awhile, usually once a year, take a real break—a total break—from their work and go on a genuine vacation. It's good for them. It's good for their work. And then we see the President of the United States trying to get away, but unable to do so. Just look at that picture in the paper. What I don't understand is, why is he smiling?"

"He wasn't smiling in that picture," interrupted Sam Donaldson.

"He was smiling on television," continued Secretary Wilmot. "At least I thought he was. But it doesn't matter. The point is, all that work. All work and no play —that's not good. Not good for the country. It's just not right. We never seem to ask this, but it's a good question, an important question, and we need to ask it: Why shouldn't the President of the United States be able to escape the tremendous, strenuous burden of his awesome responsibilities for a real vacation every year just like everyone else?"

On *The Capital Gang*, on *The McLaughlin Group*, on *Face The Nation*, and in political discussions all across the nation, the same topic kept coming up. Sitting at home watching it all, Ted Koppel was making notes for a Monday evening *Nightline* to be devoted to a discussion about whether the President of the United States should be able to take a genuine get-away-from-it-all vacation just like everyone else.

Up in New Hampshire, the President of the United States and Bill Schulz spent Sunday afternoon sitting in front of the television set drinking beer and watching the Sunday afternoon baseball game between the Baltimore Orioles and the Seattle Mariners.

And waiting for the early polling data that would tell them the public's reaction to Bill Schulz's trial balloon.

# Fifteen

"Just like everyone else"—the spin spun.

The President and Bill Schulz were back in Washington, alone in the Oval Office discussing ideas for rearranging the President's schedule to see how they might be able to leave two or three weeks open, when the President's personal secretary, Kay Bolton, buzzed the President on the intercom: "Got something here that you and Bill will want to see right away."

Kay walked into the Oval Office with a big smile across her face and a copy of *Time* magazine in her hand. She was the only other person in the world who had been informed about the President's health problem and she had also been completely briefed by the President and Schulz on what they were trying to pull off.

"Can you believe this?" she said. "Can you believe it?"

The President looked at the cover of *Time* and smiled. Then he handed it to Bill Schulz. Schulz beamed. This was the third time that Jack Newell had graced the cover of *Time*. This time the photo was just like the photo that had been in *The Washington Post* and newspapers all across the nation—the President walking out of the White House carrying an armload of work and holding it up for the cameras and looking like he was trying to force himself to smile.

The copy on the cover of *Time* read: "THE PRESIDENCY: TOO MUCH WORK & TOO LITTLE PLAY?"

Inside the cover was a message that *Time* published under the heading, "A Letter from the Publisher." Those persons whose reasons for buying a newsmagazine include the enjoyment of reading letters from the publisher would read that "for many years now" *Time* had been pondering "with increasingly more concern" the "not merely ignored, but virtually never even thought about" issue of "how economic policies, social programs, foreign affairs—indeed all issues— are affected by the fact that the nation's chief executive, our President" is unable to "periodically fully recharge his batteries" because of "exaggerated expectations" which "the public has unwittingly allowed to become a modern tradition."

"What," *Time* asked, "has made us come to expect that one man, a human being just like everyone else, is supposed to be able to operate week after week, month after month, year after year, without any *genuine* substantive physical or mental diversion while under pressures so enormous that few of us can even imagine them?"

"Surely," *Time* continued, "it should be obvious to every American who is concerned about the soundness of our government that the time has come to raise and then try to answer new questions about the Presidency." The great new question that needed to be raised and answered, said *Time*, was: "Would it not indeed be healthier for America if the President of the United States periodically, at the very least once a year, laid aside the great burdens of his office and took a genuine vacation just like everyone else does?"

*Time*, repeated *Time*, had long been pondering "such vital questions." And that is why, *Time* confessed, *Time* has always "meticulously" covered the "so-called weekend vacations" of President Newell and his predecessors "not merely to be on hand prepared to cover any news that might break during these away-from-Washington work sessions, but also, however subtly, to point out to the American public that our Presidents do not get sufficient rest, a fact which, to an extent that most of us would not care to speculate, is certainly a contributing factor to important national and international problems."

*"So it's going to be the media's idea, is it?"* Bill Schulz thought to himself as he read the "Letter from the Publisher." *"Perfect!"*

To help *Time's* readers better understand "this previously not publicly pondered issue" which "is just now surfacing in the public's mind" and which "is just now beginning to be recognized for the important questions that it raises," *Time's* "Letter from the Publisher" directed its readers to page 70 for "an incisive and provocative article" which "traces the roots of this important newly emerging public question all the way back to the vacations George Washington took whenever he felt the need to rejuvenate his perspective."

The President and Bill Schulz had barely finished looking over the *Time* piece when Kay buzzed the President again. "They're all nuts," said Kay as she came into the Oval Office. She was smiling broadly. In her hand she held a copy of *Newsweek.*

There it was on the cover. That same scene of the President leaving the White House and holding up his pile of work. Same basic photo. Just a slightly different angle. As usual, *Newsweek's* editors had made the extra effort and had managed to find a less flattering shot of the President. But the President and Schulz couldn't have asked for better cover copy.

The headline on the cover of *Newsweek* read: "IS THIS ANY WAY TO TREAT THE PRESIDENT OF THE UNITED STATES?"

The cover story began on page 48:

"As a people, we Americans pride ourselves on the esteem we all share for the office of the Presidency, if not for that office's particular occupant at any given time. We disparage, we joke about, we ridicule individual Presidents, but we stand in awe of the office itself. Have a President—any President—appear in any American city and thousands of citizens suddenly take new pride in their hometowns, as if it were being given some special blessing. Wherever the President appears, crowds gather. People wait hours just for the possibility of catching a two-second glance of 'The President Himself.' Hands reach out to touch him, as if by doing so they can touch a piece of history."

"*It's all falling in place,*" Bill Schulz thought to himself. "*It's all falling in place.*"

"We have so elevated the Presidency in our minds that we have begun to ascribe super-human qualities to the office and by extension to the person who occupies the office."

"*What bullshit,*" Jack Newell thought to himself.

"Many of the expectations we place on him are, in fact, quite super-human. We forget that, for all the majesty of the office, for all the glory and power that go with it, the individual who occupies the office at any given time is just that — an individual—merely one person, only one human being just like everyone else, with the same drives and same needs as everyone else."

"*Just like everyone else! You've got it!*" Bill Schulz said to himself.

"It is an interesting new phenomenon that Americans are suddenly—finally—asking themselves if we are harming the national interest by demanding that our Presidents be such workaholics. The American people are beginning to wonder if we have really thought as much as we say we have, and as much as we should, about the health of the office of the Presidency and the well-being of those who temporarily occupy that office. Nobody knows quite how it happened . . ."

"*Thank God they don't know how it happened,*" the President thought to himself.

". . . but today people all across America are suddenly—finally—asking themselves: Why have we selfishly expected whomever is President of the United States to do without a basic benefit that every hard working American citizen takes for granted—a genuine annual vacation? It's a good question."

*"What bullshit!"* The President thought to himself.

*"Love it!"* Bill Schulz said to himself.

Members of the Senate and the House were quoted by both *Time* and *Newsweek* as reporting that they were receiving "a heavy volume" of mail and phone calls asking why they all take real vacations when they "won't let" the President have a real vacation even though "he needs it a lot more."

"Most people think we take one every week," a congressman who asked not to be identified told *Time*.

"It's like the pay raise issue," one senator told *Newsweek*. "You just can't explain it to people. I wish the President would go visit some resort for a few weeks so people would understand that he is just as entitled to a genuine vacation as we are. I wish he'd do it. I really do. If he doesn't, Members of Congress aren't going to be able to take vacations anymore. The public won't stand for it."

It was a chorus. Just about everyone the news media quoted seemed to agree that it would be a good idea if the President of the United States took a real vacation every year "just like everyone else."

*U.S. News & World Report* didn't carry that now famous photo on its cover, but among the five articles touted on the cover banner headlines was one titled, "IS THE LACK OF PRESIDENTIAL REST UNHEALTHY FOR THE NATION AND THE WORLD?"

The now famous photo did appear on page 18, the first page of a four-page interview with the president of The American Medical Association, a psychiatrist, who took 1,200 words to say, yes, he does think that it is "unhealthy" if the United States, or any significant world power, is led by a person who never gets an authentic break from his work.

In small- and medium-sized cities across the nation newspapers began running editorials extolling the benefits of having the President of the United States get away for a genuine vacation once a year just like everyone else.

*Playboy* sent a telegram to the White House urging President Newell to take "a real vacation" and issued a news release saying they had done so. The big announcement from *Playboy* was that the Playmate in the issue after next would be quoted as saying that she would not want to marry anyone who might become President "because it's all work and no play there these days, not like it used to be, and who would want to be hitched to some guy who never gets to go on a real vacation just like everyone else?"

"Well, that ought to reduce the number of Presidential contenders from now on," said the President when he read about the telegram in the newspaper. "Say, how come nobody showed me that telegram?"

"We were afraid you'd answer it," said Kay Bolton.

"Just wait until you see *The New York Times*," said Bill Schulz. "The *Times* prefers to see where its followers and imitators are heading before it takes the lead in anything. What the *Times* is probably doing right now is trying to find some different angle that the others have overlooked or underemphasized. Then they'll stress that point and the others will pick up on it and the *Times* will be perceived as having been in the lead on all this."

Schulz was right. *The New York Times* soon joined in and endorsed the idea of a genuine get-away-from-it-all Presidential vacation in a long lead editorial:

> "Not very long ago most of us would have sneered at the idea, recently advanced by concerned members of an alert news media, that it might be healthy for the nation if the President of the United States were persuaded to set aside two or three consecutive weeks each year for a period of genuine retreat from the responsibilities and burdens of his high office. But now the public is beginning to understand that the President would be better able to gain new perspective on

the national and world problems with which he must cope if he once a year rejuvenated himself both physically and intellectually in the time-proven way—by taking a *total* break for a couple of weeks or so."

*"Fantastic!"* Bill Schulz said to himself. *"Fantastic!"*

"We don't demand that the President of the United States never sleep. Why should we demand that the President never take a *real* vacation?"

*"Incredible!"* Schulz said to himself.

"A genuine vacation for the President would provide the ideal way to guarantee invaluable experience for the Vice President. Should something ever happen to the President would not the country, and the world, feel more confident knowing that the Vice President at least had the experience of standing in for the President for at least two or three weeks each year?"

*"Are you nuts,"* President Newell said to himself.

"There is, of course, one glaring potential for abuse and note should be taken of it."

*"Uh-oh,"* Bill Schulz thought to himself.

"We must not allow gross exploitation of the possibilities for building up the public image of the Vice President . . ."

*"Not to worry,"* Schulz said to himself.

*". . .* for partisan advantages either to enhance the re-election prospects of a team approaching re-election or to launch an incumbent Vice President on a presidential campaign of his own."

*"Hum,"* Schulz said to himself.

"The Vice President must keep a low profile and concentrate on the nitty-gritty, day-to-day work of the Presidency, not the more attention-getting aspects."

*"You got it!"* Schulz said to himself.

*"Huh?"* Vice President Bates said to himself.

"A sophisticated public would demand this. President John William Newell, who probably will not be President after Inauguration Day anyhow . . ."

*"Bastards!"* The President said aloud.

**Washingtoniana**

"... needs to try to understand the new mood of the nation. He needs to dare to be bold and set an example for future Presidents by becoming the President who proves that it is not merely possible, but desirable, for the President of the United States to get away from it all and take a genuine vacation just like all the rest of us do."

The Establishment had spoken.

# Sixteen

When the President and Bill Schulz next got together back at the White House, the President happened to remark that it was odd, truly odd, that here he was President of the United States, the greatest honor in America, probably in the entire world, and what was he doing but plotting to try to escape from it. At least for awhile.

Jack Newell also remarked that half of Washington, and probably a few hundred thousand people elsewhere in the country, would absolutely love to be President. At least for awhile.

The President was in a talkative mood and he talked on and on. Mostly about how he just couldn't believe that the news media was doing exactly what Bill Schulz had predicted they would do—embracing this "just like everyone else"/ "real vacation" idea and acting as though it was really their idea and that they had discovered widespread latent public support for it. All the TV reports and newspaper articles which were reporting that the public strongly supported the idea had the effect of making the public actually strongly support it, the President observed. First they reported that this was the public's view and then it became the public's view, not the other way around, the President noted. He thought that was sort of funny. He also thought it was sort of scary.

Bill Schulz wasn't paying full attention to the President's light conversation. Let the President ponder and relish the incredible stunt that Schulz had just pulled off, Schulz himself had more important things on his mind. He had to come up with some additional clever stunts—and he had to do it quickly.

If he was to have any significant chance of becoming President of the United States himself, first he had to make sure that Jack Newell got that genuine rest he so badly needed. It appeared that this hurdle had been jumped in a fantastic public relations leap. So far, so good.

But for Schulz to realize his ambition, it wasn't enough for Jack Newell to simply remain alive. What if Bates did all right while the President was away on holiday? Not too likely, he supposed. More likely that increased exposure would harm Bates. But what if Bates did next to nothing—took a dignified low profile? Might Bates not receive favorable notice for not hamming it up? Any favorable notice for Bates would make it more difficult to dump him. Could be a real problem.

And even if the President hung in there, and even if they were able to move Bates off the ticket, there was still the problem of Stupp. If Schulz did succeed in deflecting attention away from the President, might that not create a massive news void that Herb Stupp would be only too happy to fill. Wouldn't they be handing Stupp a dangerous monopoly on news-making opportunities?

Also, of course, for Schulz to have a substantial shot at his big dream, they would have to keep the press from hounding the President while he's resting. They would have to somehow restrict the news media to limited, controlled access, leaving them little time for questioning, no real time to notice much of anything.

Because what if photos that should show the President relaxed and refreshed instead came out making him appear haggard and under stress? What if reporters interviewed him about how he's enjoying getting away from it all and something seemed fishy? What if they ended up writing stories that raised questions about the possibility that there is really something wrong with the President? If the media ever started speculating about anything like that, it would be all over.

It was like a chess game to Bill Schulz. For every move he thought of he had to think what counter moves it might open and how he would then have to cope with each possible counter move.

Schulz's thoughts suddenly returned to what the President had said just a few minutes earlier.

It hit him in a flash. Like a bolt of lightning.

Just the gimmick they needed to keep attention from focusing on the Vice President while the President gets away for his genuine rest.

Just the gimmick they needed to keep Stupp's public relations efforts in check.

Just the gimmick they needed to keep the press from nosing around too much and maybe figuring out that the President actually required this vacation that Schulz had conned the country into favoring.

The President talked on and on. Schulz let him ramble. He was barely listening. Now he was mulling over the inspiration that had just hit him. Finally, when he was satisfied that he had indeed thought of the perfect way to pull off the Presidential "just like everyone else—real vacation" while keeping the press off the President's back and keeping both Bates and Stupp in check, he interrupted the President and told him his idea.

At first, the President did what he always did when he first heard one of Bill Schulz's really wild suggestions: he shook his head and rolled his eyes.

Schulz told the President that what they needed to do was come up with some way to pick some ordinary citizen to stand in for him while he was off on vacation. Sort of an "Honorary President."

The public loves that sort of fantasy, he argued. And the news media loves writing stories about such fantasies. He reminded the President that in the early days of television and the heyday of radio there had been a very popular program called *Queen For A Day*. Some very normal housewife was treated like royalty for one day in her life and millions who were leading anything but a royal existence loved to behold it.

This sort of thing is a recurring theme, said Schulz. Americans have a thing about cheering for the little guy who, for a moment in time, gets to play the role of a big shot. That so-called average person's good fortune enables millions of other so-called average people to imagine themselves fulfilling a dream and by so doing achieve great vicarious pleasure.

People who wouldn't turn the page of their newspaper to read about a nuclear attack on the neighboring town will lap up every detail of the story about the latest lottery winner, he claimed. Doesn't put one cent in their own pocket, but they lap it up. And every day, he noted, millions of Americans watch a small handful of people win prizes on game shows. Doesn't do very much for the viewers, but millions watch programs like that for hours on end.

One out of four Americans of voting age watch *Wheel of Fortune* at least once a week, Schulz told the President. That's a higher percentage of American voters than can correctly identify Canada on an unmarked map of the world, he claimed.

Schulz made a number of other observations of a similar nature and argued that the conclusion of all this was that the American public would absolutely love the idea of having some ordinary citizen win the chance to sit in as the vacation replacement for the President of the United States.

Just for the ceremonial parts, of course. It'd be made very clear to the public that the lucky citizen who was chosen to be the honorary vacation replacement couldn't invade a foreign country or try to balance the budget or anything reckless like that.

The "Honorary President" couldn't do anything of substance—that would, of course, be unconstitutional—but he could do one hell of a lot of ceremonial things. Entertain visiting dignitaries at the White House. Do public service spots for charities. Tell the public which vegetables he likes or doesn't like. That sort of thing.

What excitement! Just think of all the publicity that would surround the selection of the lucky citizen. It would play right into the "regular guy" theme Schulz had so successfully launched for Jack Newell. It would be fun. It would create a good feeling in the country—and that could be nothing but good for an incumbent President.

And while the news media were focusing on this, they would *not* be focusing on the Stupp candidacy.

And they would *not* be focusing on the Vice President.

And they would *not* be hounding the President rigorously enough to detect anything wrong with him.

The herd instinct of the news media would, as always, take hold and the result would be that the focus of the country and perhaps the world would be on the fun and follies of some typical American citizen whom no one had ever heard of and whom everyone would afterwards quickly forget. The news media would go at it *ad nauseam.* For a few weeks— which would just happen to be the few weeks Bill Schulz and President Jack Newell needed for buying time—the "Honorary President" would be the star of the nation. He would dominate America's television screens and fill the country's newspapers. And when a few weeks passed and it was all over, this "Honorary President" would have become some sort of folk hero. And he'd be a perfect pick to deliver one of the speeches seconding the nomination of President Newell at the national convention. He'd be a nice little extra asset in the campaign. Soon he'd be forgotten and Schulz would get him some nice soft government job somewhere.

The President asked Schulz how he would pick the person who would become "Honorary President." A drawing? A contest? Bill Schulz said that was just a small detail that would work itself out. The important thing, said Schulz, was that this was an idea whose time had come.

And what did the President of the United States think of the idea of picking some ordinary citizen to fill in for him as some sort of ceremonial substitute?

"Who gives a shit?" said President Jack Newell. "Anybody would be better than 'The Jerk.' "

# Seventeen

U p went another trial balloon.
       And once again the results were nothing but remarkably favorable.

Picking an ordinary citizen to serve as "Honorary President" while the President of the United States goes off on a genuine get-away-from-it-all vacation was an absolutely splendid way to increase interest in public affairs. That, in a nutshell, was the near universal verdict of the American news media.

It was, as Yogi Berra would put it, "déjà vu all over again."

"Here we go again," Kay Bolton said aloud to no one in particular when she saw the first White House Office of Communications daily news briefs early in the morning and picked up the latest magazines. She buzzed the President on the intercom: "Got something here that you and Bill will want to see right away. Those fools in the media are at it again. You're going to die laughing. No pun intended."

"No pun intended," the President repeated with a laugh in his voice as Kay walked into the Oval Office with the daily news summary in her hand.

"Can you believe this?" she asked. "They're nuts! They're nuts! And you two are damned lucky it is not an impeachable offense to abuse freedom of the press in such an outrageous fashion."

"I think she's half serious," Bill Schulz said to the President.

"Hell, Kay," said the President, "we're just doing unto them as they have been doing unto us."

"It is funny," said Kay. "But it's kind of scary, too, don't you think?"

"Yes," said the President, "it is every bit as scary as it is funny."

The President and Bill Schulz reviewed the neatly organized collection of news reports and editorials about Schulz's idea of picking some ordinary citizen to be "Honorary President" and each of them noted with delight the theme that the news media seemed to have adopted. The news media had clearly decided that the fashionable, politically correct stand was to note the "fairness" of it.

All across America newspaper editorials and newspaper columnists and radio and television commentators were echoing this spin that Bill Schulz had put on the idea during the off-the-record background briefings: that picking an ordinary citizen to be "Honorary President" would help insure that the President and his Vice President would not receive any "publicity windfall" that could be exploited for the coming election. That is, it was "fair."

No one mentioned—because no one suspected—that it was also a clever way to deflect attention from both the Vice President and the President for awhile if you were trying to hide something.

In a lead editorial enthusiastically endorsing the idea, *The New York Times* wrote:

> "We are delighted that President John William Newell has heeded our call and has temporarily put aside his vanities and bowed to the clear wishes of the people."

"Not as delighted as we are, huh, Jack," said Bill Schulz. The President laughed.

"We feel that picking an ordinary citizen to be 'Honorary President' while the President of the United States gets some genuine R&R for a change provides a new opportunity to focus public attention on our national institutions from perhaps a new perspective."

"They're dopey," the President said to Bill Schulz. "They're just plain dopey."

"We should welcome and enjoy this entertaining way to refocus attention on the importance of citizen participation in government. It just may be the needed stimulus to get more citizens to register to vote. Let us make this a citizenship learning experience, to be sure, but let us make it a fun experience for the country, too. And let us be careful not to ruin it. Let us not permit anyone to deliberately or even inadvertently exploit it."

"Unbelievably dopey," the President remarked to Schulz. "Can't they see what you're up to?"

"You mean what *we're* up to," said Schulz. "You're a co-conspirator, you know."

"We must take care that what President Newell gets out of this is a good rest, not an opportunity for even more news coverage of the incredibly self-promoting nature he seems to have been exploiting in recent weeks. We must take care that Vice President Bates gets his helpful new experience behind the scenes, not in front of the cameras."

"Damned right we must," Schulz said to the President.

"That's the fair way to do it. That's the right way to do it. Do this right, do it fair, and the country will be well served by this historic new experiment."

"Perfect!" Bill Schulz said to the President. "This is absolutely perfect!"

"It's also absolutely ridiculous," said the President.

A reporter from *The Washington Post* was the first to ask presidential candidate Herb Stupp what he thought of the idea of picking an ordinary citizen to be "Honorary President" while President Jack Newell went off on holiday. Stupp said that what he liked about it was that "it seems fair."

# Eighteen

I t almost got out of control.

Everyone in America, it seemed, had an idea about how to pick the "Honorary President."

The National Governors' Association promptly issued a news release urging that it be done by a national lottery with each state participating in the profit in direct proportion to the number of lottery tickets sold within its borders.

The National Education Association endorsed the proposal of The National Governors' Association, but demanded that all proceeds be earmarked for increased teacher salaries.

Gamblers Anonymous issued a statement chastising both The National Governors' Association and The National Education Association for "callous disregard of the growing problem of gambling addiction among teenagers."

The National Association of Toastmasters Clubs urged a nation-wide speaking contest, to be organized and judged, of course, by its members.

The American Numismatic Association held a news conference at which its association president argued that it wasn't right to require people to pay out money to have an opportunity to become "Honorary President" because, among other things, that discriminated against "a large portion of our population who do not have sufficient spare funds to help support state-sponsored gambling."

He also argued that a speaking contest was "inappropriate" because some of our finest Presidents were not great speakers. He noted that Thomas Jefferson hated to make speeches and is remembered as a great writer, not a great speaker. That's true.

He said that if Lincoln had been judged only by those who listened to him deliver the Gettysburg Address he probably would never be selected as "Honorary President" since it was only much later, after people read and reflected upon his remarks, that anyone perceived what a great speech it was. That's not true.

It is true that immediately after delivering his remarks, Lincoln characterized his speech as "a flat failure." The nearby Harrisburg *Patriot & Union* did dismiss it as "silly remarks." The reporter for the *London Times* did call it "ludicrous" and did report that, "Anything more dull and commonplace it would not be easy to produce." And the Lincoln-hating *Chicago Times* did call it "silly, flat and dish-watery" and did denounce what they claimed was Lincoln's display of "ignorant rudeness" and "exceeding bad taste."

But lots of others called it right. *The Cincinnati Gazette* reported that the "universal encomium" for Lincoln's remarks was "the right thing in the right place, and a perfect thing in every respect." *The Providence Journal* said that one of the hardest things to do is deliver a good five-minute speech and reported: "We know not where to look for a more admirable speech than the brief one which the President made . . . thrilling words . . . the charm and power of the very highest eloquence." *The Springfield Republican* called Lincoln's speech "a perfect gem; deep in feeling, compact in thought and expression, and tasteful and elegant in every word and comma . . . verbal perfection and beauty . . . he can talk handsomely . . . a model speech. Strong feelings and a large brain were its parents." And, of course, the great orator Edward Everett, whose very long speech, the effort of his life, had preceded

Lincoln's very brief "Dedicatory Remarks" that 19th day of November in 1863, knew on the spot that it would be Lincoln's remarks, not his, that the world would much note and long remember and the very next day he sent Lincoln a note saying that he wished he had been able to express in his two hours of speaking what Lincoln had so wonderfully expressed in just a couple of minutes.

The head of The American Numismatic Association may not have had his history quite right, but in the matter of picking the "Honorary President" he did have a solution to offer. "Flip a coin," he said. "It's the American way." He said that The American Numismatic Association could arrange everything, starting with coin flips in towns and villages leading up to state-wide contests and finally a national "flip off" of the fifty state winners held on the White House lawn.

"Poor people don't have a lot of coins," shot back the Governor of Illinois on behalf of The National Governors' Association. "That's why they call them poor people."

"You only need one coin per person," rebutted the head of The American Numismatic Association. "Under our plan, all a person needs to qualify is one penny. We'd prefer, of course, that they use Indian head pennies, but any penny would do. These politicians just can't stand a system that doesn't let them milk millions from the people."

Suggesting ideas for selecting the "Honorary President" quickly became a national pastime.

The American Legion and The Veterans of Foreign Wars issued a joint statement urging that the honor go to a veteran "to recognize the invaluable contribution made to our country by its veterans and to acknowledge the nation's gratitude." Their statement included a listing of past presidents who had served in the U.S. Armed Forces.

The Farm Bureau and The Grange teamed up and issued a lengthy statement about the importance of the American farmer, complete with quotes from ten presidents about the importance of agriculture and the superiority of American farmers to any others in the world. They listed ten good reasons why picking a farmer was the best choice.

The National Committee to Preserve Social Security and Medicare jumped at the chance to send yet another mailing preying on its millions of elderly members. This one warned the poor old people that their social security payments could be "in serious jeopardy" unless they promptly sent yet another $10 to the Committee and also mailed the enclosed postcards to their two Senators and their Representative. The pre-addressed postcards contained a printed message urging the Senator or Member of the House of Representatives to see to it that a Senior Citizen was selected as "Honorary President."

The National Organization for Women (NOW) and other feminist groups pointed out that America has never had a woman President and said, "The least they can do is pick a woman for this honorary position so women in America will at least have some sort of Presidential role model." Naturally, they claimed that only they could select an appropriate woman for the role.

"Those leftist loonies would never have picked Margaret Thatcher for British Prime Minister," cracked the head of The American Conservative Union.

The "Miss America" contest found itself embroiled in an uproar when the spokesperson for the contest, asked to respond to NOW's remarks, not only agreed that it should be a woman but added that a good idea might be to simply select the new "Miss America" who was going to be crowned the following weekend.

The chief spokesperson for The Native American Rights Fund accused The National Organization for Women of "insensitivity." Said Chief Walk In The Wind: "Haven't they noticed that no Native American, male or female, has ever been President?"

"What the hell do they mean there has never been a Native American President?" raged the head of NOW. "Are they saying that for the past two hundred years the White House has been occupied by foreigners?"

"Tell that wiseass dumb shit squaw that that's exactly the point," shot back the spokesperson for The Native American

Rights Fund. "They've all been descendants of foreigners—just like her. If my ancestors had had a better immigration policy, all those guys—and her, too—they'd be Europeans!"

Chief Walk In The Wind added that he would endorse as a compromise the suggestion of The American Numismatic Association that an Indian head penny be used in a coin flip to select the "Honorary President" as long as "the Indian head coin flip is conducted for the purpose of selecting a real Indian."

The head of United Native Americans criticized him for "the shocking display of referring to 'Native Americans' as 'Indians,'" but the head of The National Indian Education Association issued a statement saying either term was perfectly acceptable.

Homosexuals and lesbians staged parades across the nation, but mostly in San Francisco and New York, demanding that the honor go to one of them "as an atonement for years of repression." The Mayor of New York agreed with them in a prepared statement in which he also appeared to apologize for being heterosexual.

The president of The National Association of Writers Clubs said that the point of the head of The American Numismatic Association was well taken—it is absolutely true that both Lincoln and Jefferson were greater writers than they were speakers. Therefore, he said, the only conclusion that could be drawn was that the most sensible way to pick an appropriate choice for "Honorary President" would be to have a national essay contest—with, of course, the topic selected and the winner chosen by The National Association of Writers Clubs.

The National Association for the Homeless criticized all the other groups. "Let someone sleep in the White House who otherwise would have to sleep on the streets," said its spokesperson. "It is outrageous to suggest that we shelter in the White House, the home that we all own, someone who already has a home. What better advocate for the nation's homeless could we have in the White House than someone who doesn't have any other home?"

There wasn't a cause in the country that didn't try to get into the act.

"Well," Herb Stupp remarked to a few close friends, "it looks like Jack Newell really stepped in it this time. He's in deep trouble unless they come up with an elderly homeless lesbian Indian farmer who served in the military and is an accomplished writer and a spellbinding speaker."

Stupp's crack popped up in the *Periscope* column in *Newsweek*.

"He's right," the President said to Bill Schulz. "This shit's out of control."

Schulz shared the President's concern and already had a solution in mind. It can't hinge on just dumb luck, he told the President. Forget any coin toss or lottery drawing. And no way could they let some advocacy group play any key role— it'd turn into a real circus. A speaking contest or an essay contest might be all right, if they had lots of time, but that approach was just too slow and too cumbersome. He advised the President to quickly appoint a Presidential Commission to decide the best approach.

"Talk about slow and cumbersome!" said the President.

Schulz said they'd stack it with close allies and those allies would do what the President and Schulz wanted and the approach taken would enjoy the prestige of having been decided upon by a Presidential Commission made up of a good number of prominent Americans. Besides, he said, he already knew the solution.

Schulz called Merv Griffin. The famous creator of some of television's most popular game shows told Schulz that he was flattered by Schulz's suggestion that his hit show *Jeopardy!* make the arrangements to screen potential candidates for "Honorary President." And he assured Schulz that he could indeed have the show on the air within two weeks.

"This is television history. We'll want to promote the hell out of this one," said Merv Griffin.

"I was hoping you'd say that," said Schulz. They both laughed.

Merv Griffin told Schulz that he'd take personal charge.

He said he would expedite matters and have his people immediately run a computer check of everyone who had ever expressed interest in appearing on *Jeopardy!* as well as everyone who had ever been recommended to *Jeopardy!* as a possible contestant.

"We have to have a good balance," said Bill Schulz.

Merv Griffin said he understood and he promised to personally screen the finalists.

The President agreed with Bill Schulz's argument that *Jeopardy!* connoted competition, competence and fairness. The perfect image. The Presidential Commission promptly announced the decision.

Herb Stupp remarked that *Jeopardy!* was "the perfect choice—after all, the whole country would be in great jeopardy if we had four more years of the current Administration."

That was not the last good political crack that Herb Stupp was to get off against Jack Newell.

But it was the *second* last one.

# Nineteen

Alex Trebek was so excited he was about to pee his pants. The smart, popular and normally smooth host of the hit television show *Jeopardy!* had suggested a small addition to the show's opening announcement to use for this very special edition of the show. He couldn't wait to hear it.

The special *Presidential Jeopardy!* had been incredibly hyped on television and on radio and in the newspapers. Alex Trebek knew that if predictions held true this show could be the most widely viewed program in television history, eclipsing both John F. Kennedy's address to the nation about the Cuban Missile Crisis and George Bush's address to the nation announcing the beginning of the U.S. military action to liberate Kuwait.

"This is *Jeopardy!*" the show's unseen announcer bellowed out in *Jeopardy!'s* trademark fashion. "Now entering the studio are today's contestants." Then the announcer paused ever so slightly and added, in his most dramatic tone: "And one of them will be the next President of the United States."

Alex Trebek smiled to himself. So did Merv Griffin. So did Bill Schulz. So did the President of the United States. From behind the curtain emerged two men, one white and one black, and a woman.

Bill Schulz poked the President and gestured toward the television screen. "Perfect!" he said. The three contestants moved swiftly to their assigned podiums.

The announcer introduced the contestants as "a school teacher from Nebraska" (the black man); "an advertising and public relations executive from Connecticut" (the woman); and "a dry-cleaning store owner from Arkansas" (the white male).

The camera moved to a long shot of Alex Trebek, then a medium shot. Viewers could see the familiar *Jeopardy!* board behind him. "Ladies and Gentlemen," he said, "Over the years there have been a lot of honors bestowed upon *Jeopardy!* and there are been some truly memorable *Jeopardy!* shows, but tonight *Jeopardy!* is participating in an historic event and the show you are about to watch will surely be the most memorable *Jeopardy!* ever."

He briefly mentioned some of the extraordinary national attention that had been focused on this particular *Jeopardy!* show and then he recounted the runoffs *Jeopardy!* had been airing all week as the lead up to this, the final prize. And then he once again explained that the producers of the program had decided that for *Presidential Jeopardy!*, because the prize was the position of "Honorary President of the United States," both the *Jeopardy!* and *Double Jeopardy!* segments would use the same six topics which the producers felt particularly relevant to the office of the Presidency.

The six subjects were: 1) American History; 2) U.S. Geography; 3) Lives of the Presidents; 4) U.S. Foreign Policy; 5) Congress; and 6) Famous Lies and Liars.

The game show host hastened to remark that the fact that they had picked "Famous Lies and Liars" as a category did not mean they were suggesting that one had to be a good liar to be President but rather that to be effective a President had to know how to spot and deal with all sorts of people.

"Couldn't you have just included that bit about liars under the 'Congress' category?" asked the dry-cleaner from Arkansas. The audience laughed and Alex Trebek couldn't suppress the grin that was breaking across his face. "I'm not going to touch that one," he said. "You sound like a President already, Hank."

The school teacher got to go first and chose "U.S. Geography."

"It's the place where the sun first strikes United States soil each day," said Alex Trebek.

"What is 'Mount Katahdin, Maine'?" said the school teacher. Correct.

"I didn't know that, and I'm from New Hampshire," said the President.

"Do we really have to make it a question?" asked the school teacher. "Can't we just give the answer?"

"No," said Alex Trebek.

"Why not?" asked the advertising and public relations executive.

"It's a long story," said Alex Trebek. "But I'm sure the people in our audience here in the studio and all across America find it reassuring to know that whichever one of you becomes 'Honorary President,' the position is going to be held by someone who doesn't hesitate to speak up and ask tough questions."

"I should make that guy an Ambassador," said President Newell. "He's a born diplomat."

The school teacher got four more questions right but then made the mistake of identifying the famous liar who directed Adolf Hitler's propaganda machine as Herbert Goebbels rather than Paul Joseph Goebbels.

"I'm sorry," said Alex Trebek. "You have the last name correct. If that's all you had said we would have accepted that. And we would have accepted 'Joseph Goebbels' as well because that's what he usually went by, although 'Paul Joseph' is more correct."

So the turn passed to the advertising and public relations executive who picked the "U.S. Presidents" category.

"This future President married a 16-year-old when he himself was only 18, the youngest age at which any President got married," said Alex Trebek.

"Who is Andrew Jackson?" she correctly responded.

She then correctly identified George Washington as the President who delivered the shortest inaugural address. She even knew that our first President's second inaugural remarks totaled only 135 words, although she didn't have to know that.

She also correctly said, "What is none?" when Alex Trebek said, "It's the number of Presidents who were an only child."

But then Alex Trebek said, "He's the President who wrote a mystery story entitled, *The President's Mystery Story,* and she said, "Who is Theodore Roosevelt?" when, of course, she should have said, "Who is Franklin Roosevelt?"

The turn then passed to the dry-cleaning store owner from Freka, Arkansas, who selected "American History."

"It's the day in 1776 that the Continental Congress adopted a resolution declaring the independence of the American colonies," said Alex Trebek.

"What is July 2nd?" answered Hank Harrison.

"What a dummy!" shouted someone in the audience.

"Thomas Jefferson's wonderful Declaration explaining the reasons why the colonies were declaring their independence was adopted on July 4th," said Alex Trebek, "but the Continental Congress actually adopted the resolution declaring independence two days before that—on July 2nd. Nice going, Hank. Not many people know that."

"I didn't know that," said the President.

When Alex Trebek said, "When American troops arrived in France in World War I, this American military officer said, 'Lafayette, we are here,'" Merv Griffin turned to a friend and said: "He'll never get this one."

"Who is Colonel Charles E. Stanton?" said Hank Harrison.

"Son of a bitch!" said Merv Griffin. "Nobody knows that!

Everybody thinks it was General Pershing. Almost every history book gets it wrong, but this guy gets it right. Incredible!"

The dry-cleaning store owner from Freka, Arkansas, rolled though every remaining question on the board. It was a dazzling performance. When *Final Presidential Jeopardy!* rolled around, his lead was so commanding that it was obvious to all that Hank Harrison would be the "Honorary President."

And on *Final Presidential Jeopardy!*, he was the only one of the three who could explain why "Dixie" is called "Dixie."

"I didn't know that," said the President.

"Good thing we never had to put you on *Jeopardy!*, huh, Jack," said Bill Schulz. "Looks like those primaries are a lot easier way to get to the White House."

The President turned and looked at Bill Schulz. "You telling me that you knew that it's because in the days before the Civil War the Citizens Bank of Louisiana used to issue bilingual currency and there were so many of its ten dollar bills in circulation with 'Dix,' the French word for 'ten,' written on them that people started calling the South 'Dixie'? You didn't know that. Shit, Jefferson Davis and Robert E. Lee and Stonewall Jackson would have missed that one. This Hank Harrison guy is something else."

Overnight the dry-cleaning store owner from Freka, Arkansas, was a national celebrity. Full television network coverage for days. *ABC News'* "Person of the Week." Cover of *Time*. Cover of *Newsweek*. Profiled on *Sixty Minutes*. The works!

And the day that Hank Harrison arrived in Washington for the "transitional" meeting with President Newell was one of the biggest media events in years. Just as Bill Schulz had predicted all along.

Asked what he thought about a dry-cleaning store owner serving as "Honorary President," President Jack Newell said: "Mr. Harrison seems like a very nice person. And obviously he is a very intelligent and very well informed person. He knows a lot about our country and it is very obvious that he loves America. I like the idea of being followed in office, even if so very temporarily, by a good patriotic American who is so smart and so nice."

Asked what he thought about a dry-cleaning store owner serving as "Honorary President," presidential candidate Herb Stupp said: "We already have someone in the White House who has been taking the country to the cleaners."

And *that* was the last good political crack that Herb Stupp was to get off against Jack Newell.

# Twenty

There is something very special about beautiful tropical islands. Something magical.

At some time or another, most people have felt this infatuation. It is a dream that has long inspired the imagination, quickened the heart and sent ships sailing. Today it sends planes flying. Off in search of idyllic islands to match the fantasy.

Fiji has such enchanted islands. More than 330 of them. Some of the most beautiful islands in the world.

The President of the United States was absolutely ecstatic that he had taken Bill Schulz's advice and selected the Fiji Islands for his just-like-everyone-else/get-away-from-it-all/ genuine vacation. It was fabulous. Just as Schulz had always described it to him. Some enchanted islands! Halfway between Hawaii and Australia and New Zealand, Fiji is the South Pacific the rest of the world dreams of. Paradise.

George Bush had visited Fiji while President and had fallen in love with the place and he had often suggested Fiji to his friends as the perfect vacation spot. Jack Newell had once heard Bush rave about Fiji at a cocktail party they both attended.

The President of Fiji had on more than one occasion extended an open invitation to President Newell to visit his country. The two men were friends. They liked and admired one another and enjoyed playing golf together. President Newell hoped that he might yet win one of their matches. They played several rounds together in Fiji but the President of the United States didn't manage to win one. The President of Fiji, a tall, powerfully-built and distinguished-looking man with a keen intellect, a winning smile and a delightful sense of humor, was one of the best golfers he had ever faced. President Newell had first met Fiji's president back when he was Prime Minister and Jack Newell was Governor of New Hampshire. Ronald Reagan had hosted a White House luncheon in his honor which Jack Newell had attended. George Bush had also had the Fijian leader to the White House, and, of course, so had Jack Newell.

President Newell knew a fair bit about Fiji. He knew that Fiji had been a British colony until 1970. He knew that this young independent Republic has Western values and South Seas charm; that English is the official language; that Fiji's people enjoy a good standard of living; and that the country's economic growth had been phenomenal in recent years.

He knew from his reading that although Fiji's population is small—about 750,000—it is multi-racial and multi-cultural. The largest group, the indigenous Fijians, make up about forty-nine percent. They are perhaps the warmest, most hospitable people in the world. James Michener once called them "the nicest people in the world."

About forty-six percent of Fiji's population are Indians, descendants of east Indian indentured laborers brought to Fiji by the British in the late nineteenth century to work the sugarcane fields. Most experts agree that the best Indian food in the world is in Fiji. The remaining five percent includes European, part-European, Chinese, Rotumans and other Pacific islanders of Polynesia, Micronesia and Melanesia. Both the indigenous Fijians and the Indians are unusually tradition-minded, which also adds a unique flavor to Fiji.

Much as Bill Schulz and George Bush had raved about it

to him, still, Fiji was even better than Jack Newell had expected. It is a land blessed with fine weather—a balmy South Seas climate with no extremes of hot or cold. A land of endless miles of magnificent white sand beaches lined with gently swaying coconut palm trees—and black sand beaches equally as stunning. A land of blue and turquoise waters so unbelievably clear they sparkle. Fabulous blue lagoons. And spectacular reefs brimming with colorful coral and dazzling tropical fish of every color of the rainbow. A land whose brilliant sunshine seems to make all colors more vibrant. A land of lofty volcanic mountains, of lush tropical vegetation, of stirring sunsets.

But it's the people that truly set Fiji apart. It really is a kinder, gentler country. In Fiji, the smiles are genuine and the hospitality comes from the heart. The President delighted in meeting the people and observing how happy and pleasant they are. "Bula," they would call out to him and "Bula" he'd call back. There was something about that warm Fijian greeting that made the day seem better.

He went off to some of Fiji's out islands in the Lau Group and discovered stunningly beautiful isolated beaches and the clearest water he had ever seen in his life. Any way he turned his eyes he felt he was looking at a postcard scene.

The President thoroughly enjoyed his own private piece of paradise. He made the Secret Service stand so far away that they complained that they had difficulty seeing him with their high power binoculars. He picnicked on uninhabited islands and made the Secret Service agents sit in boats off shore while he did so. He swam in waters of unbelievable radiance and wouldn't let the Secret Service come in the water too near to him.

The press, too, was forced to keep their distance. Most of them ended up treating the assignment as a holiday. And most of them filed such glowing reports about Fiji that the country's leading resorts became booked up two years in advance. American real estate developers rushed to Fiji to start planning new resorts.

The President also made a three-day side trip to Fiji's

nearby neighbor, the Kingdom of Tonga, Polynesia's last kingdom, which, like Fiji, is noted for its delightful climate, uncrowded and unspoiled beaches, spectacular clear water and warm, friendly people. There he became friends with two smart and charming men, the King of Tonga and His Royal Highness, the Crown Prince, who, he discovered, to his utter amazement, was more knowledgeable about military affairs than most of his advisors from the Pentagon, the NSC or the CIA.

The President was having the dream vacation of his life. Back in Washington, Hank Harrison was having the dream vacation of *his* life—living in the White House and playing at being President. It was the biggest news story since the Gulf War—near constant coverage. Hank signed all sorts of proclamations naming this day for some cause and that day for some other cause. He posed for photos with tourists in the Rose Garden. He and Mattie-Faye hosted a television special from the White House saluting top American charities. The two of them created an incredible traffic jam when they went out shopping in Washington one day. All sorts of celebrities flocked to Washington to pose for photos with Hank.

Bill Schulz reviewed the polling data every day and what he saw was a continuation of the upward movement in the President's positive ratings that had started right after the initiation of the "regular guy" campaign.

Over in the Old Executive Office Building, right next to the White House, Vice President Bernie Bates was up to his ears in an avalanche of detail work which, at Bill Schulz's urging, the President dumped on him to help keep him out of the way. He was kept out of sight and not many people asked where he was.

Bill Schulz was busier than ever. On direct orders of the President of the United States, he had been assigned to work with "Honorary President" Hank Harrison. That is, he stood behind the scenes and pulled the strings.

Whatever it was that Herb Stupp was doing, nobody seemed to care. He had virtually disappeared from the television screen and the front pages.

Bill Schulz's grand plan was going just perfect. For almost three weeks the President of the United States relaxed in Fiji and delighted in the sensational scenery, the tranquility of the tropics and the soothing serenity of the South Seas. In postcards to friends back home, the President wrote that Fiji is more than a beautiful group of islands, it is a beautiful state of mind. He wrote his friends that Fiji is "soothing to the soul."

The President hated to leave, but he had to. He felt totally refreshed. He had not felt this good in a long time. And he vowed to himself that he would return to Fiji, and Tonga, too, just as soon as he could.

# Twenty-one

On the trip back to Washington, the President stopped in Hawaii and visited CINCPAC, the Honolulu command post for all U.S. military forces in the half of the world that extends from the west coast of the U.S. mainland all the way across the Pacific Ocean and on all the way across the Indian Ocean, too, all the way to the east coast of Africa. He had also stopped at CINCPAC on his way out to Fiji. On the return trip, he took time out to speak at a Hawaii political gathering.

Then the President went on to California. First, he stopped in Los Angeles for a couple of large events, one clearly a political campaign appearance and the other supposedly an official Presidential visit.

Then he did the same thing in San Francisco. And then in Salt Lake City, Phoenix, Dallas, Denver, St. Louis, Chicago, Louisville, Columbus, and Pittsburgh, too. An eleven state campaign swing in just a few days. Only they didn't call it that.

When *Air Force One* finally touched down at Andrews Air Force Base just outside Washington, a small crowd was on hand. It was seven o'clock at night.

Hank Harrison was there. It was a dream "photo opportunity" for the news media. Bill Schulz was there, too. The smile on his face lit the darkness. Vice President Bernie Bates was also on hand.

After the arrival ceremony the President boarded *Marine One*, the Presidential helicopter. He asked Bill Schulz and Hank Harrison to join him. The Vice President promptly headed over to *Air Force Two*, which was standing by to fly him and couple of his aides to Colorado, supposedly for government business but actually to get away to his favorite trout fishing stream in the Rockies. Fifteen minutes later *Marine One* touched down on the South Lawn of the White House. The President invited Bill and Hank into the Oval Office for a chat and then later he asked them to join him upstairs in the private quarters.

He liked Hank Harrison. Like most Americans, the President had been very impressed by Hank's remarkable performance on *Presidential Jeopardy!* and when Hank had come to Washington a few weeks ago for their media event "transitional meeting" the President had made a point to have a half hour chat with the man and they had hit it off very well. For his part, Hank had long liked and admired the President.

The two of them and Bill Schulz talked about Hank's experiences as "Honorary President" and then the conversation turned to politics and the upcoming campaign. The President asked Hank to invite his wife to please join them and she did. She only stayed a short while and then she took the hint and excused herself so the three men could go back to their political conversation.

The President found himself thinking that Hank Harrison sure was a far smarter person than one would think from just looking at him. Hank was wearing a plaid shirt with a striped tie and he looked more like someone playing the role of a hick than someone playing the role of a President. The man may read a great deal, the President thought to himself, but his library obviously did not include any of those "Dress for Success" books. The President also had a positive impression of Mattie-Faye—smarter than she looks and clearly a very nice person.

The President also found himself thinking that Bill Schulz was a political genius. It seemed that every one of Bill's ideas which the President had initially viewed as absolutely nutty had proven to be strokes of political genius, including this incredible idea of having some ordinary citizen stand in as "Honorary President" while the President of the United States went away on vacation in Fiji and Tonga.

He talked about the luncheon meeting he was going to have the next day with the Speaker of the House and the Majority Leader of the Senate to discuss plans for when Congress returned to Washington following their current lengthy break. He also asked Bill and Hank to join him for breakfast in the morning. And then he excused himself.

Hank went to the Lincoln bedroom, where he and Mattie-Faye had been sleeping these past few weeks and where the President had just invited them to remain for the following week or so.

Bill Schulz headed home. On the way out, he paused in front of the Oval Office and looked in. He thought it helped to try to picture himself there.

After a shower, the President slipped into bed. He was exceptionally tired. But he felt good. For the first time in a long time he felt truly confident about the November election.

He picked up the pad and pen that he always kept on the small table at bedside and he jotted down a few quick notes about points that he wanted to cover at his breakfast meeting with Bill Schulz and his new friend, Hank Harrison, and later at his luncheon meeting with the the Speaker and the Majority Leader.

He reached for the special phone at the side of his bed and entered a code message which instructed his personal valet to wake him at 6:45 AM, the usual time. Then he closed his eyes and laid back and thought about the white sand beaches and blue lagoons of Fiji and Tonga. And then he fell asleep.

He did not wake up.

# Twenty-two

At eight thirty-three in the morning, the Presidential Press Secretary entered the news briefing room on the fourth floor in the Old Executive Office Building and walked briskly to the podium.

The room was noisy, filled with the sounds of reporters making jokes to one another about what the White House might conceivably say to try to put the best possible spin on the fact that the real President was back and ready to take over from "Honorary President" Hank Harrison.

Everyone knew that nothing much of importance had gone on while the President was off in Fiji and Tonga. After all, Jack Newell had picked the last part of July and early August for his holiday and, as everyone in the nation's capital knows, the heat and humidity are so awful in Washington at that time of year that Congress is not in session and it is difficult even to find a bureaucrat in his office.

The reporters were expecting a political show and they had a huge supply of cynicism and sarcasm ready to unleash on the Press Secretary. The Press Secretary leaned into the microphone and cleared his throat, not because he had to, but because that was his polite way of telling the noisy reporters to shut up and sit down.

"President John William Newell died in his sleep last night," he began.

A loud gasp swept the room. Then, just as quickly, the room fell silent.

The Press Secretary continued: "The President passed away at approximately 5:47 AM. Cause of death was natural causes due to an incurable disease diagnosed some months ago . . ."

Bill Schulz was standing at the side of the room. Kay Bolton had called him at home to break the news to him and Bill had rushed to the White House to try to help out. *"Oh, shit!"* he thought to himself, *"the Doc has covered his ass by getting that 'diagnosed some months ago' bit included in the statement. Can't blame him. But it could be difficult to explain."*

The Press Secretary continued: "The President was pronounced dead at 6:18 AM by White House physician Dr. Gary Nelson. The doctor had been summoned to the President's bedroom after the President's personal valet, Mike Edwards, had found the President dead after entering the room when the President had failed to respond to his repeated knocks on the door. The President's physician will be available in this room one-half hour from now to explain in greater detail and to answer questions."

That was the signal for the news media to break and file their reports and they did so in a flash.

Of course *CNN* was covering the news conference live and therefore television and radio programs across America and across the world were alert to the news and were already interrupting their programming to carry news flashes announcing the death of the President of the United States.

The Vice President of the United States was not yet aware of what had happened. He was off fishing in a remote mountain stream in Colorado. It was easy enough to get a message to him. The Secret Service was, of course, accompanying him and, of course, they have superb communications equipment. But for some reason the message was not passed to him. Not for awhile. Later, an internal Secret Service report would fault this too long delay and the head of the Secret Service would be criticized for it. But it wouldn't bother him very much. Like his older brother he was used to being criticized a good bit. His older brother was Chief Justice of the United States.

"Maybe it's best for Jack," Bill Schulz remarked to his wife, Lynne, whom he had brought along to the White House with him so that the two of them could assist Kay Bolton with all the arrangements. "He goes out a winner. The public will quickly forget that his popularity was down only a few months ago and most people will say good things about him and they'll look back upon his time here with some fondness."

"That'd be nice," said Lynne Schulz.

"Yeah, nice for him," said Bill Schulz. "Awful for me. I've lost my best friend. And with the same blow I've also lost my life's dream."

# Twenty-three

L ess than fifteen minutes following the White House announcement of the death of President John William Newell, something very unusual happened.

Two miles away from the White House, in a building across from the Capitol Building, a building that few Americans even recognize when they pass by it or see it in a photo, the reporters who cover the Supreme Court of the United States were summoned to the Court's news conference room for what they were informed in the summoning phone calls would be "a major announcement of historic proportions."

The Court's Press Secretary didn't know it then, but over the course of the next couple of days he would ride to media fame and would later make a fortune by quitting the Court to give speeches at law firm dinners and county law societies across the nation. For now, however, all he knew was that he was to go to the podium and simply introduce the Chief Justice.

A side door to the large conference room opened and the Chief Justice of the United States emerged and began to walk slowly toward the podium. Richard E. Stowe looked like a Chief Justice. Tall and athletic, Hollywood-handsome, with a ruby complexion and wavy gray hair and steel gray eyes, the

67-year-old former Governor of Kansas projected authority. Everyone in the crowded room rose the instant he entered. He was wearing his black judicial robe. As he neared the podium, he reached into his pocket and took out a piece of paper.

The Press Secretary announced that the Chief Justice would make a brief statement and take no questions until a second news conference that he expected to schedule within a couple more hours. Chief Justice Stowe reached into another pocket and took out his glasses and stepped forward to the podium. He unfolded his glasses and put them on. Then he began to read from the piece of paper.

The assembled reporters couldn't believe what they were hearing. It was the most startling news that any of the reporters who cover the Supreme Court had ever heard in this historic building.

The Chief Justice of the United States announced that the Supreme Court had just issued an injunction forbidding the administering of the oath of Presidential office "pending further review."

He said that the Court's order stemmed from "deliberations" of the members of the Court "over a considerable period of time." He offered no explanation.

He promised that the Court would "within a few hours" hand down a very important ruling "clarifying" this "unusual but necessary" action.

And then he turned and walked away. Reporters shouted questions at him, but he did not respond. He just kept walking. Straight out of the room. Straight into history.

# Twenty-four

"Who the hell is President?" asked the Speaker of the House when he heard the news about the Supreme Court injunction.

"If the Vice President isn't, then you are, sir," said his top aide.

"But they didn't say that the Vice President isn't, did they?" asked the Speaker.

"No, I guess they didn't say," said the Speaker's aide.

The Majority Leader of the Senate called the Speaker immediately after the Chief Justice's announcement and the two Congressional leaders agreed to get together as quickly as possible in the Speaker's office to talk things over.

"There is no President of the United States at this moment," said the Majority Leader, as he entered the Speaker's private office and proceeded to sit down in the big red leather wing-back chair that he always favored. "I can't believe this is happening."

"Well, what the hell exactly is the problem?" asked the Speaker.

"It's a legal problem, sir," said one of his aides.

The Speaker glared at his aide. "What kind of a legal problem?"

The aide replied that nobody seemed to know. The Speaker and Majority Leader told their aides that they wanted to speak with the Vice President right away.

"What if the Russians attacked?" asked the Majority Leader.

"They'd get their ass kicked," said one of the aides who had accompanied him to the meeting.

That happened to be the same conclusion the Russians themselves had come to during their most recent secret War Games. Both the Speaker and the Majority Leader had been told that by the CIA but neither one of them remembered. The aide knew it, however.

The two Congressional leaders could not get through to the Vice President. From the White House, from the Vice President's office, even from the F.B.I., they got the same response: "The Secret Service advises us that the Vice President is in seclusion."

"His secretary said she thought he was fishing," said the Speaker.

"Jerk!" said the Majority Leader.

CNN had switched to live coverage of the State Department's briefing for the foreign press and the Speaker and Majority Leader watched attentively.

"We do not want to say that this is a constitutional crisis," the State Department spokesperson was saying. "We do not want to speculate on how this situation might be adversely affecting the national security interests of the United States. We do not want to say that the Government of the United States is in a state of total confusion."

"Dumb shit!" said the Speaker, as he looked at the television screen.

"Who's President?" asked one of the foreign journalists.

The State Department spokesman scratched his head. "We're not quite sure," he replied.

"Do you have one?" asked another foreign journalist.

"One what?" asked the State Department spokesperson.

"President," said the foreign journalist.

"I think so," said the State Department spokesperson.

"Would you venture a guess as to who it might be?" asked another foreign journalist.

"We would rather not speculate on that at this time," said the State Department spokesperson.

"That idiot is saying the worst possible things any fool could say under these delicate circumstances," said the Majority Leader.

"Maybe we should find Al Haig and ask him to dash over to the White House and say that he's in charge," said the top aide to the Majority Leader. "He'd like that, I'm sure. Better to have someone than no one."

"This isn't funny," said the top aide to the Speaker. "It's the biggest crisis since, ah, since . . ."

"The last one," said the top aide to the Majority Leader.

CNN soon switched to the Pentagon for live coverage of the daily news briefing by the Pentagon spokesperson.

"Are U.S. military forces on special alert?" asked The Washington Post.

"U.S. military forces are always on special alert," responded the Pentagon spokesperson.

"Have there been any extraordinary precautions taken as a result of the death of the Commander in Chief?" asked ABC News.

"Whenever extraordinary circumstances occur, appropriate steps are taken," answered the Pentagon spokesperson.

"Could you tell us what those steps are?" asked CBS News.

"As you know, it is our policy not to unduly elaborate on such sensitive topics," responded the Pentagon spokesperson.

"At least this guy is smart enough not to say anything," said the Speaker.

"Who's finger is on the button?" asked The Washington Times.

"Button?" said the Pentagon spokesperson.

"The nuclear button," said The Washington Times. "Who controls it, right now, this minute, as we speak?"

"We would rather not speculate on that at this time," said the Pentagon spokesperson.

"Shit!" said the Majority Leader.

The Speaker and the Majority Leader called the Chief Justice. They were told that the Chief Justice was in Court and would call back just as soon as he could. They got the same response when they tried to get through to each of the other eight justices.

While the Speaker and the Majority Leader were in Washington for their scheduled luncheon meeting with the President, the rest of Congress was still in recess. All across the country, every one of the other 99 Senators and every one of the other 434 members of the House of Representatives was being asked by the news media and by their constituents for an explanation of what was going on.

None of them had the faintest idea. Which, however, restrained very few of them from rushing in and offering up an explanation. Which, of course, compounded the confusion.

"Yes, it is unusual for the Supreme Court to enjoin against the oath of office being taken, but things similar to this have happened before in American history, so there is no ground for concern," explained the Yale Ph.D. senior Senator from Connecticut, one of the nation's best-known U.S. Senators, in an interview with NBC News. "It is just a small technical matter."

That reassuring response to NBC News' question about how worried people should be about this strange development was promptly picked up by the wire services and broadcast constantly over television and radio. The Senator's comment seemed to offer some relief for his congressional colleagues. Within twenty minutes more than a majority of the Members of the House of Representatives and forty-five of the one hundred members of the Senate quickly echoed the famous Senator's remarks and the air waves were filled with their comments. That seemed to reassure the country.

The senior Senator from Connecticut was, however, quite wrong. Nothing like what was happening had ever before occurred in American history. Neither he nor those who echoed him knew what they were talking about. Which, of course, was not all that surprising.

Within an hour the air waves were carrying statements by all sorts of obscure professors from all sorts of prominent universities—and every one of them was saying that the Members of Congress did not know what they were talking about and had made historically inaccurate and misleading statements. More than one professor ventured the opinion that the Members of Congress had conspired to spread false information. "There is a massive cover up going on here," said one professor. Many others said they agreed with his assessment. It was an easy way to get on television and get quoted in the newspapers.

"Everything is under control," CNN quoted the chairman of the House Judiciary Committee as saying to his colleagues who had talked with him. "The Vice President is in charge and everything is under control. There is absolutely no doubt about that."

"It's a Court coup," said the junior Senator from Texas, a man known for his colorful and occasionally extreme statements. CNN and all three networks carried his remark.

The Secretary of Defense finally gave up trying to get through to the Vice President and decided to contact the Speaker and Majority Leader. A few minutes later, the Secretary of State did the same.

"The CIA informs us that all the key players of the Russian regime are assembled in the Kremlin for an emergency meeting," the Secretary of Defense told the two Congressional leaders.

"So what's so unusual about that?" said the Majority Leader. "That's to be expected."

"Our best Russian analysts advise us that this new gang in the Kremlin is likely to become convinced that this is some sort of trick on our part," said the Secretary of Defense. "They might even conclude that it's a clever prelude to a U.S. military strike."

"Holy shit!" said the Majority Leader.

"The President is dead!" shouted the Speaker. "Are you telling us those idiots think that a dead President is going to launch an attack against Russia?"

"We have no way of knowing what they are thinking," said the Secretary of Defense. "All we know for sure is that they are highly suspicious. You must bear in mind that we're not dealing with the Yeltsin group anymore. And, of course, it's not even like it used to be with the Gorbachev group. These new hard-liners are very strange characters. They're worse than the old hard-liners ever were, at least in the sense that they're so damned difficult to figure out. Remember, they're not very smart either. I'm telling you, the CIA sure called it right last year when it referred to their seizure of power as the 'Coup of the Kooks.' Anyhow, our sources tell us that the new Russian leadership seems convinced that our shots are really being called by Bill Schulz."

"Who?" said the Speaker.

"Schulz. Bill Schulz. The President's buddy," said the Majority Leader.

"This is ridiculous," said the Speaker.

"Absolutely ridiculous," agreed the Majority Leader.

When the Secretary of State called, he told the two congressional leaders that he was being inundated with calls from all major U.S. allies and reported that some of them, the best informed ones, were horrified at the thought of Bates' taking the reins of government.

"They are wondering why Bates has not been seen," said the Secretary of State. "A few of them are asking me if there is anything to this claim of a 'Court coup.' Actually, they kind of hope it's true."

The two Congressional leaders again telephoned the Chief Justice. And once again they were told that the Chief Justice was in Court and would call back just as soon as he could and, no, under no circumstances could he be interrupted. They then sat down and talked over the situation with their top aides. After they did that, and after having conferred once more with both the Secretary of Defense and the Secretary of State, they were still confused.

The Speaker of the House and the Majority Leader of the Senate put their heads together—and the score was nothing to nothing. They had no idea what to make of the situation. Not the faintest. Thus they had no idea what to do. Not the foggiest. So they decided to do what "decision-makers" in Washington so often decide to do when they can't think of anything sensible to do: They scheduled a news conference.

# Twenty-five

A t the Kremlin, the new Russian Dictator and the top echelon of the Russian leadership were meeting in emergency session to ponder the new developments in the United States. Immediately upon hearing the announcement of the death of President Newell, the Russian Dictator, or Chairman of the People's Council, as he preferred to be called, had summoned to the Kremlin all the key players of the People's Council, the group of cronies who had worked with him ten months earlier in pulling off the successful coup that had ousted all reformers and restored Russia to true dictatorship after first subjecting it to considerable bloodshed.

Calling such a meeting was, of course, the sort of move that should be standard precautionary procedure under such circumstances and at first none of the men who had helped make possible the "Coup of the Kooks" gave it all that much thought. But as they sat in the Kremlin watching CNN together lots of strange thoughts started going through lots of strange minds.

"It is trick! It is trick!" shouted the Chief of Intelligence. "The American imperialists are plotting to attack."

The Russian Dictator leaped to his feet. "They're going to attack us?" he asked in a frantic tone. "Holy shit! What the hell are we doing here? Let's get to the bunkers."

"No, not us, Comrade Chairman," said the Chief of Intelligence in a tone that displayed more than a touch of impatience with his boss. "Not us."

"Is true," said the head of the KGB. The Russians had two intelligence operations now. The old KGB, which stands for Committee For State Security in Russian, and the new Intelligence Committee, headed by the Chief of Intelligence, a man the CIA believed to be the kookiest of any of the ring leaders involved in the "Coup of the Kooks." The KGB had responsibility for domestic repression and shared in responsibility for foreign intelligence operations, but the Intelligence Committee was clearly becoming dominant in foreign intelligence authority, if not yet skill.

"The warmonger imperialists are scheming to grab control of the Middle East oil," said the Chief of Intelligence. "Newell probably resisted the idea and the capitalist lords who control the multi-national corporations have had him done away with. And now Bates is going to carry out the instructions of these greedy capitalists."

"They don't do away with their leaders like that, you idiot," said the Minister for Transportation. "We're the ones who do that."

The Russian Dictator glared at him.

"We have seen no movement of U.S. military forces which would lend credence to such conjecture," said the commander of the Red Army.

"Of course not, you damn fool!" said the Chief of Intelligence. "What kind of a trick would it be if they did something like that which made it easy for us to see what they are up to?"

"Is that pig Newell really dead?" asked the Minister for Shipping. The Chief of Intelligence said he did not know and it would not surprise him one bit if Newell was really alive and the announcement of his death was just a trick to provide extra surprise cover for the oil grab.

"That's not intelligence," said the Minister for Civil Aviation. "That is sheer stupidity. The imperialists couldn't get away with pretending that the President had died. The American public would never tolerate such a thing."

"Fool!" shouted the Minister for Defense. "Fool! Look at the plots they have been engaging in lately. These reports we have that Newell was secretly negotiating to appear on *Wheel of Fortune* and soap operas, too. Going on vacation in Fiji. Making some CIA agent dry-cleaner 'Honorary President.' Is all part of very clever plot."

"He is not CIA agent," said the head of the KGB. "This Hank Harrison guy really is just a dry-cleaner. We can't figure it out."

"Ha!" said the Minister for Defense. "They have fooled even the KGB. They wouldn't have fooled the old KGB. You lost all the really good people when Yeltsin forced Gorbachev to decimate it. It's going to take you another year or more to rebuild it into a first-rate operation again. So, listen to me. Newell is not dead, Comrades. Is damned plot. If we do not stop them, the imperialists are going to control most of the world's oil supply and we'll be sitting here in Moscow watching the snow fall and freezing our asses off."

"On what pretense would the Americans try to steal the Middle East oil?" asked the Minister for Oil and Gas. "Would not they be afraid of what the Union of Sovereign States might do?"

They still liked to refer to themselves as the Union of Sovereign States. They seemed to feel it gave them some legitimacy. Everyone else just called them the Russians. Or the Commies. Lots of people thought the CIA had hit it right on the mark and simply referred to them as "the kooks in the Kremlin."

Following the August 1991 Revolution the Soviet Union had disintegrated right in front of the eyes of the whole world, with all but two of the so-called Republics of the so-called Union of Soviet Socialist Republics ultimately declaring their independence. The Union of Sovereign States that had followed was sort of a common market of countries which had in common the fact that they didn't have a whole lot of things to sell to one another, a loose confederation governed by the State Council, the Inter-Republic Economic Committee, the Council of the Republics, the Council of the Union and other committees and councils so numerous that listing them all seemed to require a small-sized phone book. Within six months after the "Coup of the Kooks," ten of the fifteen "Republics" of the former Soviet Union were back together again doing business as the Union of Sovereign States. Statues of Lenin and Stalin and, of course, the Chairman of the People's Council, too, were the rage of the land.

"Do not underestimate the imperialists," said the Minister for Transportation. "They have smart weapons. We have stupid weapons."

"The American public would never tolerate such unprovoked aggression," said the Minister for Oil and Gas. "Not even for cheaper oil."

"Bullshit, Comrade" said the Minister for Defense, "Is brilliant political stroke. Just like war against Iraq. Just like the secret way they saved Yeltsin and Gorbachev from the August 1991 attempted liberation."

"What secret way?" asked the Minister for Oil and Gas.

"You idiot!" shouted the Minister for Defense. "They didn't tell us how they did it. It was a secret plot!"

"And now they have another brilliant scheme like the kind they used to stop Iraq and like the kind they used to block the August 1991 attempted liberation?" asked the Russian Dictator.

"Except better this time," said the Minister for Defense. "They are going to steal the Middle East oil. All they have to do is find a pretense. That is easy. Then Newell will go on television and say that Japan's economy is totally at the mercy of the United States because America will control 90% of Japan's sources of oil. He will boast that America will be fair in supplying oil to Japan only if Japan changes its restrictive trade practices. The American public will fall for this trick."

"They are all imperialists, the Americans," said the Minister for Oil and Gas.

"The yen will suddenly lose much of its value and Americans will suddenly be buying televisions and VCRs and nice new cars at great bargain prices," continued The Minister for Defense. "Newell can promise a Lexus in every garage. The Japanese will not know what to do. They have no military, no weapons. They will bow and do whatever is necessary to please the Americans and Newell will get all the credit. Comrades, there can be no doubt. The pig Newell is alive. This is Schulz's most devious stunt ever. Damn, it's brilliant!"

"Where is the Vice President? And what is this business that their stooge Supreme Court is up to?" asked The Minister for Coal.

"The Vice President is just a decoration," said the Minister for Defense. "He's not in charge anyhow. It is this CIA accomplice Schulz who is deciding everything."

"Exactly," said the head of the KGB.

"But Schulz is an ally of the dead President, not of the Vice President," said the Minister for Shipping. "He could be out of power now because the Vice President is in charge."

"Comrade, do you not understand the ways of the imperialists?" asked the Chief of Intelligence. "Newell is alive. That is why the Vice President has not been sworn in. The Court is under orders from the CIA. Is big plot. Is clever trick."

"I say that no one is in charge there," said the Minister for Fisheries. "This could be a great opportunity for the Union of Sovereign States. Why don't we make some mischief and have some fun?"

"That's exactly what the imperialists want us to believe," said the Chief of Intelligence "They are pretending that they are in a state of confusion in order to confuse us."

"What if they are not pretending?" asked the Minister for Fisheries.

"Fool!" said the Chief of Intelligence. "The Court is involved just to confuse some of the opposition in Congress. Very tricky. It is Schulz's work. He is the most devious American strategist. He is enemy of the people. We must stop him. He is dangerous capitalist warmonger imperialist aggressor.

At this very moment he is plotting to beat the hell out of Iraq or Iran. Or maybe Libya. Maybe all of them at the same time. Then the imperialists in the U.S. government and the greedy capitalist who control the big oil companies will conspire together to reduce gasoline prices so low that they'll be almost giving it away in the weeks just before Election Day. Then after the election, when Newell is safely back in the White House for four more years, they will price gouge and take massive profits from the pocketbooks of the American workers. Very clever."

"I am going to call Newell and warn him that the Union of Sovereign States will not sit idly by while the Americans engage in an imperialistic adventure," said the Russian Dictator.

"But, Comrade Chairman," said the Minister for Medicine, "that's the problem. We really do not know whether Newell is alive or dead. If he is alive, he is not going to respond to you because he is pretending that he is dead. And if he is dead, well, then we do not know who is in charge. This Bill Schulz and his fellow conspirators are doing a very clever job of blurring the picture."

"What the hell are we going to do?" asked the Minister for Defense. "Maybe we should issue a strong statement warning the Americans against any imperialistic adventure. Maybe we should put all Russian military forces on full alert."

"You mean to say all the military forces of the Union of Sovereign States," corrected the Russian Dictator. "Let's think about it," he added. "But first let's just watch CNN some more and see what's going on."

# Twenty-six

B ernie Bates was getting angrier and angrier by the minute. "I'm President, dammit," he shouted into the phone.

On the other end of the line the Speaker of the House and the Majority Leader of the Senate looked at one another and shook their heads. "I'm sorry," said the Speaker, "but you have not taken the oath of office. You are not at this moment President."

"The Constitution doesn't say a damn thing about taking any oath of office," shouted the Vice President. "It says that the Vice President becomes President. Period. So I'm President. Right now. It so happens that my legal advisor was part of our fishing trip party and he has briefed me. He says I'm President right now—no doubt about it."

"But the Supreme Court has enjoined you against taking the oath of office and that means you are not President," said the Majority Leader.

"It does like hell," said the Vice President, "Listen, I've got it right here in front of me, the 25th Amendment. It says, right here in section one, quote: In case of the removal of the President from office or of his death or resignation, the Vice President shall become President. End of quote. That's what it says."

"I'm sorry," said the Majority Leader, "but it's the Supreme Court that interprets the Constitution, not the Vice President, and sure as hell not some staff guy."

"Are you thick or something?" asked the Vice President. "I'm not Vice President. I'm President. It does not take any court interpretation to figure out that when the Constitution says that upon the President's death the Vice President becomes President then, dammit, I'm President."

"You're the one who's thick," shot back the Majority Leader. "The Supreme Court has enjoined you from taking the oath. How many times do you have to hear it before it sinks in?"

"I am ordering you as President of the United States to cease and desist from obstructing the Constitution of the United States."

"Sorry, Bernie," said the Speaker, "but like the Majority Leader said, you and your fishing buddy don't interpret the Constitution, the Supreme Court does. We cannot recognize you as President until you have taken the oath of office."

"I'm going to remember this," said Bates. "I am going to have the FBI and maybe the CIA investigate what the hell has been going on. The Secret Service deliberately kept word of the death of the President from reaching me for as long as they could. That is very strange. Very strange."

"What are you talking about?" asked the Majority Leader.

"Oh, you know," said Bates. "Both of you know. I can tell. You're in on it with the Chief Justice. It's no coincidence that his brother heads the Secret Service. And now you two are trying to pull this crap about not recognizing me as President when you know damned well that I am."

"Look," said the Speaker, "We told you how it is. You have to take the oath of office and you have not done so and you cannot do so until the Court lifts its injunction. And, besides, what's this crap about the CIA? You ought to know that the CIA is forbidden by law to conduct domestic operations against American citizens. What the hell kind of a President would you be if you don't even know something so basic?"

"I do not need to take an oath to become President," shouted Bates. "I have been President from the moment Newell died."

"Cut the crap," said the Majority Leader. "Everybody knows that the President takes an oath of office. Shit, little kids know that. Now the Speaker and I represent one co-equal branch of government and the Supreme Court represents another co-equal branch of government and two out of three of the branches of government say that you are not at this moment President. So by a 2-to-1 margin you are not President. It's that simple. Now I suggest you drop it and maybe in another couple hours, maybe even less than that, the Court will explain what this little technicality was and we can all go on from there."

"You didn't hear me, did you?" asked Bates. "I said I am not going to forget this. You two jerks had better read the Constitution."

"Of all people to be calling anyone a jerk," said the Speaker.

"Check out the Constitution," said Bates. "You might want to know that the penalty for treason is death."

"That does it," said the Majority Leader. He slammed down the telephone.

# Twenty-seven

The Speaker of the House and the Majority Leader of the Senate had held joint news conferences many times over the years, but never before a crowd as big as the one gathered before them on this occasion.

The Speaker began the news conference by reading a brief opening statement on behalf of the two of them. In the statement, the two Congressional leaders praised President John William Newell as a good and decent person and said that the American people would mourn his loss.

They also said that on behalf of the Congress of the United States they wanted to assure the American people that there was no need for concern about the events unfolding in Washington. They labeled the Supreme Court's statement "a minor technicality" and said that "a full and satisfactory explanation" would be forthcoming from the Court very shortly. They said that they had been "in consultation" with the Vice President and the Secretary of Defense and the Secretary of State.

Their statement ended: "Your government is functioning well, as historically it always has when the torch is passed."

"Who's holding the torch right now?" shouted NBC News.

"Pardon?" said the Majority Leader.

"The torch," said NBC News. "You said the torch has been passed. To whom? Who's in charge?"

"There is no need for concern," said the Majority Leader. "That's all we need to say at this time."

"Why did you say 'Vice President'?" asked The Miami Herald. "Why do you not refer to Mr. Bates as 'President'?"

"It is simply a matter that the oath of office has not been administered due to the Court's injunction because of this minor technicality, whatever it is," said the Speaker. "I think we have fully explained that there is no need for concern and that a full and satisfactory explanation will be forthcoming very shortly."

"Why don't you give us a 'full and satisfactory explanation' right now?" asked CBS News. The crowd laughed.

"I think we have said all that needs to be said at this point in time to assure the American people that things are perfectly normal," said the Majority Leader.

"Are you saying that what is going on right now is 'perfectly normal'?" asked The New York Times.

"Well, normal for Washington," said the Majority Leader. The crowd laughed again. He had not intended that to be funny.

"Did you say that the government is functioning well and historically it always has at such times," asked ABC News, "or did you claim that the government is functioning as well as it always does at such times? There's a difference."

"This is not a time for semantics," said the Speaker.

"Are you aware that Vice President Bates' office has issued a statement announcing that he is on his way back from his fishing trip in Colorado and that he will be holding a news conference at Andrews Air Force Base upon his arrival there?" asked The Chicago Tribune.

"No, neither the Speaker nor I were aware of that," said the Majority Leader.

"Didn't he mention that when you spoke with him?" asked The Dallas Morning News.

"I don't recall," said the Speaker.

"Why is Bates taking so long to return to Washington?" asked The Baltimore Sun.

"I have no idea," said the Speaker.

"What does Mr. Bates think of this unusual development?" asked CNN.

"He'll undoubtedly expand upon that at his news conference," said the Majority Leader.

"One of your colleagues, the junior senator from Texas, is referring to this unusual development as 'a Court coup.' Would both of you please comment on that?" asked The Wall Street Journal.

"Well," said the Majority Leader, "my dear friend the distinguished junior senator from Texas has made many important contributions to the Senate and to the Government of the United States and he has represented the good people of Texas exceedingly well in the Senate and many times he has pointed out to me and his other colleagues insights we might otherwise not have arrived at and often I agree with him fully and most of the time I mostly agree with him, but I would not characterize this minor technical delay in quite that fashion."

" 'A Court coup'? It's the nuttiest thing I've ever heard of," said the Speaker.

"Now just wait a minute," said the Majority Leader. "Some of your folks over in the lower house have been saying some pretty dumb things about all this."

"It was a member of the upper house who made that dumb statement that what is going on here isn't all that unusual and has happened before," said the Speaker.

"Are you calling me dumb?" asked the Majority Leader.

"Not you," said the Speaker. "I'm talking about your colleague from Connecticut. The one who is always bragging about his Ph.D. and then had to be corrected by all those professors because he doesn't know what he's talking about."

"Are you two speaking on behalf of Congress?" asked The Des Moines Register.

"Of course we are," said the Majority Leader.

"Yeah, we're the congressional leaders," said the Speaker.

"Have you polled the members of Congress to get an idea of their views about these unusual developments?" asked The Philadelphia Inquirer.

"You can't conduct a poll at a time like this!" said the Majority Leader.

"Then how do you know you are speaking for them?" asked The Philadelphia Inquirer.

"Oh, come on," said the Speaker.

"Mr. Speaker," said The Atlanta Constitution, "when you and the Majority Leader were arguing a moment ago . . ."

"We weren't arguing," interrupted the Speaker.

"You could have fooled us," continued The Atlanta Constitution, "but here's the question: You said that for the Senator from Connecticut to claim that this whole strange development is really nothing all that unusual is quote dumb unquote. That's the word you used—'dumb.' Now, isn't that exactly what you and the Majority Leader are saying here, too? There is no real difference between what he said and what you are now saying, is there? So if you characterize it as 'dumb' when he says it, how would you characterize it when you say it?"

The Speaker and the Majority Leader were stunned. The room fell silent and the point sunk in. A ripple of laughter began to race across the room.

"I think perhaps the Majority Leader might want to respond to that question," said the Speaker.

"No," said the Majority Leader. "He asked you."

Loud laughter suddenly filled the room.

The faces of the Speaker and the Majority Leader turned pale white. They looked frightened. They were trapped and they knew it. And they knew the reporters knew it. What really frightened them was that they knew that millions of Americans were watching this latest Congressional disaster on television in living color. They could imagine how awful they must look on the close-ups. And they knew the media smelled blood and would now go for their throats.

"Mr. Speaker," said The Atlanta Constitution, "would you please answer my question?"

The Speaker sputtered and hemmed and hawed. "Answer the question!" shouted another reporter from the back of the room. "Answer the question!" shouted another. And another. And another.

Finally the Speaker spoke: "There is a time to speak and there is a time to remain silent. This is a time to be silent."

The mocking moans and derisive laughter were deafening.

"You mean you guys called a news conference to tell us this is a time for silence?" asked The Washington Post.

And once again laughter filled the room.

"Are you going to schedule more silent news conferences?" asked The Orlando Sentinel. Once again everyone broke out laughing. Everyone, that is, except the Speaker and the Majority Leader and most of their staff members. Even a few of their staff couldn't help laughing.

"What are the funeral arrangements for President Newell?" asked The Los Angeles Times.

When it was obvious that neither the Speaker nor the Majority Leader had any idea about the funeral arrangements, the Russian Dictator and the members of his inner circle exchanged knowing glances. The Chief of Intelligence pointed at the television screen and smiled and said, "You do not make funeral arrangements for someone who is not dead. The imperialists have given it away. Newell is not dead."

"What is the purpose of this news conference?" asked The New Orleans Times Picayune.

"Oh, come on," said the Majority Leader.

"Who's on first?" asked The Chicago Tribune.

"What?" asked the Speaker.

"You know," said The Chicago Tribune. "This whole business sounds like that old Abbot and Costello 'Who's on first?' comedy routine."

"Are you comparing the Speaker and I to Abbot and Costello?" asked the Majority Leader in an indignant tone.

"Who's on first?" repeated The Chicago Tribune. "Just tell us who's on first! You don't even have to tell us who's on second. Just tell us who's in charge. Who is running the show? Don't you know?"

At the Kremlin, the Russian Dictator pointed to the television screen and said, "They do sort of remind you of Abbot and Costello, don't they?"

"Comrade Chairman," said the Minister for Defense. "They cannot be as stupid as they are pretending to be. The Chief of Intelligence is right: it is trick."

"But it really does sort of remind you of that Abbot and Costello routine," said the Russian Dictator. "That is one of my favorite American comedy skits. Of course you have to be very familiar with American baseball to understand why it's so funny. I like baseball. I like it a lot. We should take it up. Make it our national game. In fact, I believe we invented it. Somebody check that out. I'm pretty sure we invented baseball."

"This no joke, Comrades," said Russia's Chief of Intelligence. "This bold political stroke. This most clever American gambit we have ever faced."

# Twenty-eight

The plane carrying Vice President Bernie Bates back to Washington and his scheduled news conference at Andrews Air Force Base was still on the ground at the Denver airport more than an hour after the Vice President had finally arrived there by car from his favorite Rocky Mountain fishing retreat. He was told that there were "technical problems."

He didn't believe it. Just as a couple hours earlier he had not believed that they could not obtain an acceptable helicopter and had to take a car to the Denver airport. Finally, he started screaming insults at his Secret Service escorts and he threatened to fire each of them if his plane did not take off within ten minutes. Which, as it turned out, was just about how much longer they planned to delay him.

In Washington, in the Speaker's Office on Capitol Hill, the Speaker and the Majority Leader and their top aides were sitting around cursing the news media. The first thing they had done upon returning to the office following their disastrous news conference had been to call Kay Bolton and find out the funeral arrangements and instruct their staffs to inform all Members of Congress of the details.

Across the way from the Capitol building, not much more than the length of a football field away, the Supreme Court of the United States was meeting. Only the nine justices were present. No court clerks. No stenographers. Just the nine persons who constitute the third branch of the government of the United States. They had been meeting for almost two hours.

"Of course I agree he's a jerk, perhaps he's even a danger to the Republic," said Justice Wayne DeHond, "but I just don't see how we can get away with ruling that Bates is not President."

"Remember, the Speaker is next in line after Bates and he's no prize, either," said Justice Lonny Dolin.

"If Newell and the Speaker were of the same party, maybe we could get away with making the Speaker President," said Justice John Considine, "but if we try to take control of the White House away from one party and give it to the other there will be riots in the streets. It's just too extreme. I can't believe the mess we've gotten ourselves into. And there's no way out without our looking really stupid with this injunction bit. I can't believe we all agreed to do this. I know that it is what we agreed to, but, oh God, this is incredible!"

Chief Justice Stowe stood up from his chair and started pacing the room. "We can't chicken out now," he said. "We've already issued the injunction. We've got to hang in there. It's what we all swore to that night at *Joe & Mo's*. Swore to! And we've talked about it lots of times since then. Maybe not in the detail that we all now wish we had, but we swore that we would stop Bates from ever sitting in the White House no matter how we had to do it. We agreed that if anything ever happened to Jack Newell, we'd issue an injunction against Bates' taking the oath of office and somehow rationalize having the Presidential succession process pass over him. I know it seemed a lot easier over drinks and dinner than it is now that we face the consequences of our action, but, folks, there's no turning back. If we back off now and let Bates take the White House, we will all be in really deep shit. We could all be impeached. And my brother could go to jail if it ever came out what he has done to keep the news of the President's death from reaching Bates when it should have. I can only guess what he may be doing at this very moment to further obstruct Bates. All I know is that he assured me that he would put every possible obstruction in Bates' path to give us time to do what we have to do."

"The obstruction we're talking about here is obstruction of justice," said Justice David Lovenheim. All nine of them suddenly had pained expressions on their faces. But no one said anything in response. Plotting about getting rid of Bates had been fun to do. Facing up to it wasn't.

"I'm afraid I agree with Justice Considine," said Justice Vince Gerace. "We can't take the White House away from one party and give it to the opposition party."

"Ah, shit, the Electoral College has done that before," said Justice Tom Gosdeck. "There's precedent."

Chief Justice Stowe excused himself for a few minutes and left the room to make a private phone call. He called Bill Schulz.

"What the hell are you people up to?" asked Schulz.

"Come on, Bill," said the Chief Justice. "You know I am not at liberty to discuss the deliberations of the Court. Listen, I need to ask you a question. To which Party, if any, does this Hank Harrison guy belong?"

"He's of the President's Party," said Bill Schulz. "Why? Who cares?"

"Are you positive?" asked the Chief Justice. Bill Schulz said he was absolutely positive. Hank had told him. And so had Merv Griffin. And he had personally checked it out, too.

The Chief Justice thanked Schulz and put down the phone and returned to his meeting. As he walked back into the conference room, he announced: "OK, I've got it. No problem. We're going to make this Hank Harrison guy President. It's only for a few months, anyhow."

"What the hell!" said the other eight Justices of the Supreme Court of the United States almost in unison.

# Twenty-nine

The constitutional law problem the Justices of the Supreme Court faced was the fact that the 25th Amendment to the Constitution of the United States explicitly states, right there in Section One: "In case of the removal of the President from office or of his death or resignation, the Vice President shall become President."

Law doesn't come any more clear than that.

They had often discussed the 25th Amendment at their *Joe & Mo's* sessions over the years and all nine of the Justices agreed that this little understood amendment, adopted in 1967, carried with it the seeds of political chaos. It was, in the view of some of them, a constitutional crisis waiting to happen.

It is Section Two of the 25th Amendment that provides that, "Whenever there is a vacancy in the office of the Vice President, the President shall nominate a Vice President who shall take office upon confirmation by a majority vote of both Houses of Congress."

Until the 25th Amendment was adopted in 1967, the Presidency was purely an elective office. To become President you had to have been elected President or elected Vice President. Not any more.

Lots of critics argued at the time of adoption that it was a bad idea to create the possibility of someone's being appointed Vice President and then become President upon the death or resignation of the President. To an obscure Congressman from Michigan named Gerald R. Ford who supported the proposal it proved to be a godsend.

But while the gist of Section Two is pretty well understood and now generally, although somewhat reluctantly, accepted, Section Three and Section Four of the 25th Amendment are not at all well known or understood. And Sections Three and Four are cause for grave concern.

Section Three provides that: "Whenever the President transmits to the President pro tempore of the Senate and the Speaker of the House of Representatives his written declaration that he is unable to discharge the powers and duties of his office, and until he transmits to them a written declaration to the contrary, such powers and duties shall be discharged by the Vice President as Acting President."

Which means, of course, that if a President of the United States decides that there are some difficult decisions coming up, he could, if he wished, simply send a note to those two people and then sit back and let the Vice President make the difficult decisions and take all the flak and then when things got better, he could simply retake the reins by revoking his note.

That may not be very likely to happen. However, it is permissible. Perhaps not likely—but definitely possible.

But it is Section Four that is truly dangerous. Incredibly dangerous. It is an inducement to destabilize the government of the United States. It is an invitation to create chaos. It is a blueprint for a constitutionally acceptable coup d'etat.

Section Four states: "Whenever the Vice President and a majority of either the principal officers of the executive department or of such other body as Congress may by law provide, transmit to the President pro tempore of the Senate and the Speaker of the House of Representatives their written declaration that the President is unable to discharge the powers and duties of his office, the Vice President shall immediately assume the powers and duties of the office as Acting President."

It is *presumed* that "the principal officers of the executive department" refers to the Cabinet. But that is not at all clear.

So there you have it: If the Vice President of the United States can convince a majority of the Cabinet—or a majority of *such other body* as Congress has set up—to join with him in signing a letter *claiming* that the President is not up to the office—presto!—the Vice President becomes Acting President. Immediately!

There is no requirement of medical evidence. No requirement of psychiatric evidence. No requirement for any supporting evidence whatsoever! The only prerequisite is that the claim be made. Section Four of the 25th Amendment requires nothing more than that.

Just make the charge. And down goes the President of the United States.

Under Section Four, a Congress strongly hostile to a President could conspire with the Vice President to strip the President of the United States of all his power and authority without Impeachment—and even without the Cabinet's participation. All they would need do is first select some stacked group and then designate it as the "such other body." It could, if they wished, consist of only two persons. Maybe even only one. And then the Vice President and that stacked *such other body* would simply need to make the claim and the Vice President would instantly become Acting President.

Those who turn a blind eye to the dangers inherent in the 25th Amendment argue that there is sufficient security against such a coup. But the only security system is blind faith that Congress and whoever is Vice President are above doing anything so sneaky. Some security!

Section Four does provide that if the President transmits to these same two Congressional figures "his written declaration that no inability exists, he shall resume the powers and duties of his office *unless* the Vice President and a majority of either the principal officers of the executive department or of such other body as Congress may by law provide, transmit within four days to the President pro tempore of the Senate and the Speaker of the House of Representatives their written declaration that the President is unable to discharge the powers and duties of his office."

But what if within four days the Vice President and his co-conspirators do reiterate their claim? Then, according to Section Four, "Congress shall decide the issue, assembling within forty-eight hours for that purpose if not in session.

In the meantime, thanks to the 25th Amendment, a Vice President and a couple of co-conspirators would have seized temporary control of the executive branch of the government of the United States.

Which, of course, means, among other things, that a devious conniver would be Commander-in-Chief of the most powerful military force in the history of the world. Empowered to send armies marching. Empowered to press the nuclear button.

If within twenty-one days from the day the second claim of Presidential inability has been made, or within twenty-one days from the forty-eight hours within which Congress is required to assemble, Congress "determines by a two-thirds vote of both Houses that the President is unable to discharge the powers and duties of his office, the Vice President shall continue to discharge the same as Acting President; otherwise the President shall resume the powers and duties of his office."

Thus, a Vice President, aided by a couple of co-conspirators, could seize control of the powers and duties of the Presidency with no need to support his claim that the President is "unable," while the President of the United States, on the other hand, must convince Congress that he is able.

Under the 25th Amendment, the President of the United States is presumed guilty if charged. In no other instance in American law is an American citizen presumed guilty. Every other American is *always* presumed innocent. Not the President.

The judgement as to whether the President of the United States is able or unable to discharge his duties is entirely a political judgement. The 25th Amendment provides no definition of inability or disability. It does not even instruct or authorize Congress to do so. No being burdened with proof here!

And what if a sleazy Vice President and a couple of co-conspirators put the country through such a disruptive ordeal and then Congress upheld the President as able to perform—what would prevent them from trying again the next year or the next month or even the next day? Nothing. Could they really do it over and over? According to the 25th Amendment, yes.

Those who turn a blind eye to the dangers inherent in the 25th Amendment argue that aroused public opinion would prevent a Vice President and the Cabinet or "other such group" from daring to seize power from a President who is physically and mentally able. But public opinion can be manipulated. And, of course, public opinion can be ignored.

"Here's my plan," Chief Justice Stowe said to his colleagues on the Court. "We zap Bernie Bates by zapping the 25th Amendment."

"Huh?" said Justice Dolin.

"We will write an opinion that says that the 25th Amendment was imperfectly adopted," said the Chief Justice. "We'll say that we have good cause to believe that there were procedural flaws in enough states to render the adoption imperfect."

"What procedural flaws?" asked Justice James White.

"I didn't say that there *were* procedural flaws," said the Chief Justice, "I said that we will *say* that there were."

"You mean," said Justice Lovenheim, "that we'll just state that as a fact and gamble that if pressed we can come up with some claims and arguments to justify our having thrown out an amendment to the Constitution?"

"Exactly," said the Chief Justice.

"I like it," said Justice Gosdeck.

"Me, too," said Justice White.

"Think we can get away with it?" asked Justice Dolin.

"Of course we can get away with it," said the Chief Justice. "It's simple, really, if you just stop to think about it."

"Simple?" asked Justice Fred Holbrook.

"To get away with it all we need do is dare to do it," said the Chief Justice. "It's that simple."

"What you are saying," said Justice DeHond, "is we can rule any damned way we want because there is no appealing a decision by the Supreme Court."

"Exactly," said the Chief Justice.

"Wait a minute," said Justice Dolin. "We're not omnipotent, much as you and I might like to think that. Remember, Congress could pass a law in a matter of hours superseding us and the President could sign it into law in a flash."

"What President?" said the Chief Justice. "What President?"

"Fantastic!" said Justice White.

"Well, Congress could quickly propose a new Constitutional Amendment and the states could quickly adopt it," said Justice Dolin.

"Quickly?" said the Chief Justice. "The Presidential election would have come and gone long before Congress and the states could move a new Amendment. And Bernie Bates would not be running for President as the incumbent. Got it?"

"Holy shit!" said Justice Gosdeck. "We're in control. We're in total control. This is great!"

"I'm not sure I follow this," said Justice Dolin. "If we throw out the 25th Amendment, and I've said for years that it's a latent threat to the stability of the Republic, that doesn't make this Hank Harrison guy President. Bates is still in line under what existed prior to adoption of the 25th Amendment. Everybody knows that."

"Lonny," said the Chief Justice, "you know, I know, we all know, that the issue of Presidential succession is perhaps the most murky constitutional issue in American history. One of the reasons the 25th Amendment was adopted was because of the uneasiness surrounding the fact that the issue of Presidential succession had been determined by statute and precedent when a whole lot of constitutional scholars, many of us included, felt that statute and precedent are insufficient and constitutionally unacceptable because it is a matter that requires a directive from the Constitution."

"Still," said Justice Considine, "those statutes and those precedents do exist. They are part of the history. Are you suggesting we cast those aside, too?"

"The first time a President died in office," said Chief Justice Stowe, "there was quite an uproar when the Vice President decided to take the oath of office. It was back in 1841. William Henry Harrison died after only a month in office and John Tyler was Vice President. Tyler's action, what those of us in the constitutional law field now refer to as 'The Tyler Precedent,' was so controversial and contrary to prevailing interpretation of the Constitution that Congress felt it had to step in by specifically passing a measure recognizing Tyler as President. Of course that very act was of dubious constitutionality because the Constitution assigned no such authority to Congress."

"You're right," said Justice DeHond. "Presidential succession has been a murky issue throughout American history. But by far the most murky aspect of it is the matter of Presidential inability or disability. When President James Garfield was shot by an assassin in 1881 he lingered some 80 days during which he performed only one official act, the signing of an extradition paper—while Vice President Chester Arthur did nothing. Absolutely nothing. And when President Woodow Wilson suffered a severe stroke in 1919 his wife and the Presidential assistants she favored ran the Presidency until he recovered."

"Presidents Eisenhower, Kennedy and Johnson each had written understandings dictating powers to be enjoyed by their Vice President in the event of Presidential incapacity," said the Chief Justice, "yet they had no constitutional authority to do so."

"What's the point?" asked Justice Dolin.

"The point is," said Chief Justice Stowe, "the Republic needs a Constitutional Amendment regarding the issue of Presidential succession that does not deal with the matter of Presidential inability or disability in a manner fraught with the danger of instability and chaos, as is presently the case. And we can force it to happen. We would be doing the Republic a noble service."

"But how do we make this dry-cleaner *Jeopardy!* star President?" asked Justice White.

"When we rule that the 25th Amendment was imperfectly adopted, and therefore null and void," said the Chief Justice, "we will also declare that those who had argued for a constitutional amendment to resolve the issue of Presidential succession were right. Remember, there were a lot of very prestigious groups and figures who argued that, including the American Bar Association, the American Association of Law Schools, the bar associations of many states and a number of persons who had served as Attorney General. We'll explain this in our decision and say that therefore we find ourselves in a situation in which there is no constitutionally proper method of Presidential succession."

"Neat!" said Justice Gosdeck.

"What the hell does that mean?" asked Justice Gerace.

"It means," said the Chief Justice, "that for the present, and until a new constitutional amendment is properly adopted, we must rely solely upon the intentions of the Founding Fathers."

"And the Founding Fathers want the dry-cleaner from *Jeopardy!*, right?" said Justice Dolin.

"Ah, but that's a problem, too, isn't it?" said Chief Justice Stowe. "The Framers of the Constitution really were not very clear on this issue."

"And so?" asked Justice Holbrook.

"We will say that the Constitution of the United States is based to a large extent on the tradition of common law," said the Chief Justice.

"To most people, that would sound rather familiar," said Justice DeHond.

"And, therefore, reasonable," said Justice Dolin.

"Exactly," said the Chief Justice.

And that is how, a few hours following the death of President John William Newell, the Supreme Court of the United States ruled that Hank Harrison of Freka, Arkansas, was legally President of the United States.

Because, as Americans have always known, and as the Supreme Court of the United States now reaffirmed in its historic decision: "Possession is nine-tenths of the law."

# Thirty

As *Air Force Two* rolled to a stop at Andrews Air Force Base outside Washington, Bernie Bates stood up and put on his suit coat.

He felt great inside. He had spent much of the flight from Denver thinking of the scores he would soon settle. That would be his first priority as President, he promised himself.

He was annoyed that all the plane's telephones and fax machines and telecopy systems—in short, everything that kept them in contact with the outside world—had gone out just as they were lifting off from Denver. He felt certain that the Secret Service was supposed to have back-up equipment available for such an emergency, but they said they couldn't do anything about the problem. It was something he probably should have someone check into, but he was confident that wouldn't ever be a problem aboard *Air Force One.*

He expected to walk swiftly down the steps and then quickly over to the familiar nearby building to meet the assembled news media for a news conference. There he would affirm that he was in charge and ask the American people for their prayers and support as he began to lead the nation as its new President.

Glancing out the airplane window, he saw a huge throng

of news reporters and television cameras assembled near the bottom of the stairs. It didn't surprise him or phase him. After all, he thought, they were probably so anxious to talk with the new President of the United States that they couldn't bear to wait for him at the small news conference room. Besides, there was clearly such an overflow crowd of them that they couldn't all squeeze into that room anyhow.

As the plane door was opening, he ran through his usual nervous ritual habit. He unbuttoned his suit coat button and then quickly buttoned it again. He shook his arms slightly and then tugged on his suit coat. He tightened his tie and straightened it. He also reminded himself to look somber.

He walked briskly down the steps of *Air Force Two.* In just under twenty seconds he was standing on the pavement at the bottom of the steps. One of the Secret Service agents who had preceded him down the steps came up to him and led him to a podium that stood on a red carpet next to the plane. With all the reporters shouting at once he found it impossible to understand what they were asking. He leaned forward and, as was his habit, he placed his left hand at the bottom of the microphone. "I want to reassure the American people that all is well," he began.

"What the hell!" exclaimed the Speaker of the House of Representatives as he watched live television coverage of the Vice President's arrival.

Bernie Bates was perplexed by all the puzzled looks that appeared on the faces before him. "Our system is functioning well," he continued, "as historically it always does at such times."

"What the hell!" exclaimed the Majority Leader of the United States Senate. He, too, was watching the live television coverage. And he, too, couldn't believe what he was hearing from the mouth of Bernie Bates.

"This is a time for all Americans to unite and think of the good of the country," said the Vice President. The puzzled expressions on the faces he was looking at made him still a bit more uncomfortable. He attributed it to his new status and he thought to himself that even he had underestimated just how in awe of the President of the United States people are at moments of such historic importance. He decided to shorten his remarks.

"Let us extend our sympathy to the family of President Newell," he said. "May God bless President Newell and keep him. He would, I know, ask your support and your prayers for the new President."

"*I never would have guessed he'd take it like this,*" Chief Justice Stowe thought to himself.

At the White House, President Hank Harrison turned to Mattie-Faye and said, "Maybe the guy's not as bad as I have been hearing."

Bill Schulz didn't know what to think.

Bates continued: "President Newell's guidance has meant, and shall always mean, so much to me. I want to continue in a spirit of cooperation that would make him proud. Thank you."

"Don't you think *you* should be President?" shouted ABC News.

The Vice President looked at ABC News and gave the news media a piece of visual and sound that they would use over and over and over for a long time to come. With a quizzical expression on his face, the Vice President looked straight into the cameras and said: "I am President." Then he turned and started walking toward his waiting limousine.

"Are you saying that you have not heard the news that the Supreme Court has declared that the dry-cleaner from Arkansas is legally President of the United States?" shouted Newsweek.

The Vice President turned to the Secret Service agent next to him and said: "These press guys are always trying to make wiseass jokes. Nothing is sacred to them. Not even the death of a President."

NBC News was closer to the Vice President. And NBC News repeated the question: "Are you saying that you have not heard the news that the Supreme Court has declared that Hank Harrison is legally President of the United States?"

Vice President Bates stopped dead in his tracks. "What

are you doing?" he said in a tone that reeked of impatience and contempt.

Then someone whom he recognized as a White House Deputy Press Secretary handed him the text of the *Associated Press* wire story about the Court's decision and said that he needed to read it immediately.

It was quite a scene. A scene that the American people would long remember.

Later that day and for days to come the news media would run the "I am President" excerpt over and over followed by one of the "Are you saying that you have not heard?" clips. And then they'd follow that with the really good stuff. Well, some of the really good stuff. Accompanied by some bleeping sounds to block out the foul language.

The Vice President of the United States jumped up and down. He ranted and raved. He pushed a television camera technician and it looked like he gave serious consideration to punching one of the news reporters. And he said some very, very foul things.

The Speaker of the House asked his aide to contact their friends in the news media to find out exactly what Bates had been saying about him in the portions that were covered with block-out bleeps. The Majority Leader of the Senate did the same. So did the Chief Justice. So did his brother, the head of the U.S. Secret Service. And so did lots of other people in the high circles of power in Washington.

Secret Service agents had to virtually push Bates into his limousine. They ignored his orders to take him directly to the White House. Instead, they took him to the Vice Presidential residence.

"You're fired!" Bates shouted at the Secret Service agents as they dropped him at his front door. "All of you. You're all fired!"

"Sorry, Mr. Vice President," said one of the agents, "but you do not have authority to fire us."

Bates shouted something obscene and angrily kicked his foot at nothing in particular. Then he walked into the Vice Presidential residence and slammed the door.

# Thirty-one

Within minutes of being informed of the Supreme Court's surprise decision, Hank Harrison summoned to the White House a group of advisors he felt he should meet with immediately—the White House Chief of Staff, the Secretary of State, the Secretary of Defense, the National Security Advisor, the Director of the Central Intelligence Agency and the Attorney General.

Also sitting in at the meeting, at the suggestion of Kay Bolton, was Bill Schulz.

As soon as they all arrived he arranged a ceremony at which Chief Justice Stowe administered the oath of office to him as Mattie-Faye held the Bible upon which he placed his hand. He made sure that the official swearing-in photos released to the news media by the White House showed in the background and at his side these familiar faces of key Newell Administration figures.

After the swearing-in, which was held in the Oval Office, he had everyone sit down and he asked them to please offer any advice they might have.

"This is an unprecedented constitutional crisis," said the Attorney General. "We can expect the Vice President to make an immediate appeal through the courts."

"About a matter on which the Supreme Court has already ruled?" said Bill Schulz. "No way!"

"Then Bates may move to have Congress impeach," said the Attorney General. "Get them to throw out Mr. Harrison here and hand over to Bates what he, and, frankly, many others, believe is properly his."

"It's President Harrison," said the Secretary of Defense. "Not 'Mr. Harrison here.' "

"After all those foul things 'The Jerk' called the Speaker and the Majority Leader on national television?" said Schulz. "No way is Congress going to lift a finger for him. They'll give him the finger."

"Our allies need reassurance," said the Secretary of State.

"Why the hell do you people at State worry so damn much about reassuring everybody else," said the Director of the CIA. "Why don't they worry about reassuring us?"

"How the hell can they reassure us?" snapped the Secretary of State. "We're the ones who suddenly find ourselves being run by a dry-cleaner."

Everybody, especially the Secretary of State, cringed.

"What I meant . . ."

"You are both right," said President Hank Harrison. "It is true that we need to let the American people and the world know that, however unusual this development might be, the government of the United States remains sound and stable and there are no other big surprises coming down the pipe. To that end, and with your concurrence and the concurrence of others with whom I intend to speak within the next hour or so, I want to announce that the entire Cabinet and all other key appointments of President Newell shall remain in place and that it is my intention that this be so until the American people have once again elected a President. I shall also announce that both the domestic policies and the foreign policy of the Newell Administration shall continue as they were."

"That would be a big help, sir," said the Secretary of State.

"It is also true," said Hank Harrison, "that State does worry too much about what others think. Let's change that.

We'll make our decisions. We'll announce them. We'll explain them. But we shall *not* apologize for doing anything we think is in the national best interest of the United States. And not only shall we cease apologizing, we shall cease sounding like we are apologizing."

Everyone present in the Oval Office was surprised by Hank Harrison's assertiveness. Every one of them was also impressed.

"The Russians could be a big problem, Mr. President," said the Director of the CIA. It was the first time since the swearing-in ceremony that anyone besides the Chief Justice had referred to Hank Harrison as "Mr. President."

"How so?" asked Hank Harrison.

"Our sources indicate that the Russian leadership believes that President Newell is still alive and that the events they and the rest of the world have been witnessing may be some sort of clever prelude to a U.S. military operation. They think we're going to steal the Middle East oil and then stick it to the Japanese by making their economy totally dependent upon us."

"That's a hell of a good idea!" said Bill Schulz. He noticed that Hank Harrison grinned when he said that.

"They think it's your idea," the CIA Director told Schulz.

"How reliable are your sources?" asked President Harrison.

"Very," said the Director of the CIA.

"I'll vouch for that," said the Secretary of State.

"You don't have to," said the Director of the CIA.

"Let's discuss this," said President Harrison. "I would like each of you to suggest how you think we should deal with this Russian paranoia."

Everyone in the room, but one, either made a suggestion or endorsed someone else's suggestion.

The Secretary of State suggested that Hank immediately pick up the telephone and call the Russian Dictator and tell him that he was aware that the Russians are concerned that the United States might be up to some surprise military maneuver and then reassure him that this was not at all the case. The Director of the CIA argued that such a move would compromise and endanger U.S. intelligence sources inside the Kremlin.

The Secretary of Defense suggested that Hank Harrison immediately summon the Russian Ambassador to the meeting so all of them together could reassure him that President Harrison was making no changes in U.S.-Russian relations. The National Security Advisor suggested that while the Russian Ambassador was present among them they say certain things as a way to subtly send a signal that the Russians had no cause for concern.

The Attorney General suggested that the Russian Ambassador be shown the body of President Newell. "We can think of some excuse for doing so. Shouldn't be too difficult. Maybe say we are all going to pay our special respects and invite him to join us. He'll see that President Newell is indeed dead and that will be the end of this little problem."

Hank Harrison had already mentioned that he intended to briefly address the nation and say what he had told this group about continuing the policies and personnel of the Newell Administration. The White House Chief of Staff suggested that a special point be made in the speech to communicate to the Russian leadership that they have no need for concern.

President Harrison looked at Bill Schulz. "You are the only one who has not either made a suggestion or commented on the suggestion of anyone else," he said.

"I have a question," said Bill Schulz.

"Go ahead," said President Harrison.

"Have the Russians sent a message expressing condolences on the loss of Jack Newell?" asked Schulz.

"Good question," said Hank Harrison. It turned out that the Russians had not. The group speculated that the Russians had not done so because they did not believe Newell was dead and they intended the absence of a condolence message to be interpreted as a signal to Washington that they were on to the trick.

"It seems to me," said Bill Schulz, "that proper courtesy dictates that the Russians express their condolences first. Before we worry about their silly conjectures. It's their move, not ours."

"I couldn't agree more," said the new President of the United States. "If the Russians want to wait until after they have witnessed President Newell's funeral before they communicate with us, so be it. Let's just keep our eyes on them."

"I have something else I'd like to say," said Bill Schulz.

Everyone was anxious to listen to the man whose views the new President had just so decisively embraced. "I have taken the liberty of conducting some public opinion polling," said Schulz. "I think you might all be interested in what it shows."

"I'll bet it's very interesting," said the Chief of Staff.

"The American people are nervous about having someone so unexperienced sitting in the White House," he began. "That's not very surprising, of course."

"Doesn't surprise me," said Hank Harrison. "I'll bet I'm more nervous about it than they are." The group laughed.

"What's truly interesting," continued Schulz, "is that the polling data suggest that those who will want to do so might find it difficult to sustain the present storm of controversy."

"Could you be more specific?" asked the Attorney General.

"Well," said Schulz, "your lawyer and legislator friends may go bonkers over this, but 73% of the public agrees with the proposition that 'Possession is 9/10ths of the law' is sound legal reasoning and a proper interpretation of the United States Constitution."

"That's amazing!" said the Chief of Staff.

"Yes, it is," said Schulz. "The data also reveals that, while a bit nervous about it, the public accepts Hank Harrison as President of the United States. People buy the argument that what the Supreme Court says is 'the law of the land' and since they have said he is President, that's that. End of argument. It really won't matter who screams and hollers."

"Very interesting," said the Secretary of Defense.

"Looks to me like there's no need to get too uptight about anything," said Schulz. "We have no concern about the Judicial branch. They're the ones who made this happen. And we have no concern about the Congressional branch. 'The Jerk' took care of that for us by his performance at Andrews."

"Anything in the poll that would really surprise us?" asked the Secretary of State.

"I don't know if this should surprise you or not," said Schulz, "but it does reveal that the public finds it quite comforting that Hark Harrison finished first on *Presidential Jeopardy!* It turns out that 87% of the American public do not believe that anyone in Congress or anyone in the Cabinet would have won if they had gone on *Presidential Jeopardy!*"

"What does the poll show about Bates?" asked the Chief of Staff.

Bill Schulz smiled. "This is the best poll I have ever seen about him. It shows that the public now thinks he's a jerk."

"What do you think, Mr. President?" asked the Attorney General.

"About the Vice President?" asked Hank Harrison.

"No, not about him," said the Attorney General. "What do think about, well, you know, all these interesting developments?"

"I think this will put those Adams folks in their place," said President Hank Harrison.

No one understood what he meant.

And no one asked him to explain.

# Thirty-two

The funeral for President John William Newell was, of course, a most solemn affair. His two sons and daughter and his brother and sister led the funeral procession on foot. Directly behind the family were President Hank Harrison, Vice President Bernie Bates, the Speaker of the House, the Majority Leader of the Senate, the Justices of the Supreme Court and the members of the Cabinet. And behind them was an assemblage of heads of state from all parts of the world. And further back, behind them, were all sorts of famous Americans. And, of course, Members of Congress.

From the Rotunda of the U.S. Capitol Building they proceeded to Constitution Avenue, then down Pennsylvania Avenue, passing in front of the White House, then turning left at 17th Street by the side of the Old Executive Office Building. As they made a right turn back on to Constitution Avenue just about everyone looked off to the left at the view of the Washington Monument and, across the Tidal Basin, the Jefferson Memorial. They walked down Constitution Avenue to 23rd Street, where they turned left. In front of them was a side view of the Lincoln Memorial. They proceeded around half the circle by the Lincoln Memorial until they reached

Arlington Memorial Bridge, where they crossed the Potomac to Arlington National Cemetery. There the Bishop of Manchester, New Hampshire, delivered the final benediction and President John William Newell was laid to rest. The entire funeral ceremony took nearly four hours.

As he had previously agreed, following the funeral President Hank Harrison met back at the White House with a group of Party leaders that the Party Chairman had brought along with him. It was to be a very short meeting. Hank Harrison knew that the Party Chairman was one of the Vice President's closest friends and advisors and he pretty much knew what to expect from him.

The Party Chairman began by thanking Hank for agreeing to meet with him and his "delegation." He said he had requested the meeting to discuss "this peculiar crisis situation" and "perhaps find some solutions that could be beneficial for all concerned parties."

He praised Hank for the "dignified and courteous" manner in which he had conducted himself "during this awkward constitutional crisis." He said that he knew from observing Hank during this "troublesome" period, and before that during his days as "Honorary President" and as a contestant on the special *Presidential Jeopardy!*, that Hank was "a fine patriotic American who certainly understands the importance of putting America's interest ahead of, well, the temptation of selfishness and personal aggrandizement."

The Party Chairman told Hank that he was "absolutely certain" that the American people "will remember you with great affection" and "always be grateful to you" for "doing the right thing, the right thing for America." Then he handed Hank Harrison five pieces of paper. It was the text of a resignation speech.

President Harrison took the five sheets of paper and leaned back in his seat. He read them very carefully. When he finished, he leaned forward and looked at the Party Chairman. "Do you want me to correct the spelling errors?" he asked.

"Oh, no, no, that won't be necessary," said the Party Chairman.

"Then for what other possible reason would you hand me such a foolish piece of writing?" asked President Harrison.

The Party Chairman was livid. "Now look here," he said, "Bernie Bates is the one who is supposed to be President. You can't just come into the White House and be a squatter or something. This is the most ridiculous thing I have ever heard of. The most ridiculous thing any of us have ever heard of, right folks?"

Somewhat sheepishly the people in his "delegation" nodded their heads in agreement.

"I can understand that you don't like the way things have worked out," said Hank Harrison, "but that's the way things have worked out. I didn't do it. It wasn't my idea. I'm sort of an innocent victim and I just have to make the best of it."

"*You're* the victim!" exclaimed the Party Chairman. "That's the dumbest damn thing I've ever heard."

"Is that all?" asked President Harrison.

"Look, I'm sorry," said the Party Chairman. "Let's be reasonable. We have a proposal."

"Sure, you want me to resign," said Hank Harrison, "so Bernie Bates and you can run things."

"Just hear me out," said the Party Chairman. "We can re-do that speech. Add your own personal touches. That would be fine, I'm sure. Then we'll make you a big star at the convention. Big star. We'll have you give one of the main seconding speeches for Bernie. You'll be on national television."

"I'm on national television all the time now," said Hank Harrison. "Don't you watch?"

"Later, we'll name you to a nice post," said the Party Chairman, ignoring the fact that already in their brief conversation Hank Harrison had twice now deftly made a fool of him. "Not anything too hard. Hell, we'll create a new position just for you. Something you can do from Arkansas. You'll be set. Everything will work out just fine."

President Harrison stood up. As if it were an involuntary reaction, everyone else in the Oval Office stood up, too. Hank walked over to the Party Chairman. He looked him straight in the eyes and smiled. "Nice of you to come by," he said. "We'll have to do this again sometime." He put his arm on the Party Chairman's shoulder and started walking him to the door.

"Folks," he said to the group, "if we were in Freka, Arkansas, and you were dropping off your laundry or dry-cleaning I'm sure I could find the time to have a much longer chat with you, but I am sure you all understand that when you are President of the United States there are some pretty big demands upon your time. So I guess it's time to say good-bye for now."

"I resent this," said the Party Chairman. "You can't get away with this. Bernie Bates is supposed to be President."

"It was supposed to rain today, but it didn't, did it?" said Hank Harrison.

"You are not supposed to be President, Bernie is," repeated the Party Chairman.

"Now, now," said Hank Harrison. "All of us know enough about American government to understand that I am President at least until Inauguration Day. And that doesn't roll around until January 20th. So let's be friends, OK? It'd be more fun. For all of us."

One of the members of the group said "OK." The Party Chairman got red in the face.

"What did you mean, 'at least until Inauguration Day'?" asked the Party Chairman. "That makes it sound like you want to run for President."

"Of course I do," said Hank Harrison. "I like the job."

"This is ridiculous," said the Party Chairman.

"It pays well, too," said Hank Harrison.

"You've got to be joking," said the Party Chairman.

"And Mattie-Faye loves the house," Hank continued in an amiable tone of voice.

"OK, be cute," said the Party Chairman. "Blow your big opportunity. Just let me ask you a couple of quick questions that might help you re-think things."

"Go ahead," said Hank.

"Do you have any idea how much each side spends in a presidential election?" asked the Party Chairman.

"I probably have a fair idea," answered Hank.

"I don't think you do," said the Party Chairman. "Most people don't. I got my big start in presidential politics back in the 1988 campaign. Back in those days it cost Bush eighty-eight million seven hundred fifty-two thousand five hundred twenty-two dollars. And it cost Michael Dukakis eighty-seven million nine hundred twenty-five thousand two hundred thirty-seven dollars just to lose. And the price has been sky-rocketing every since. Now tell me, Mr. Harrison, can your friends and neighbors in Freka, Arkansas, raise a hundred and twenty-five million dollars for you real quick? That's what I figure you'd need if you want to run for President. At least $125 million. How much of it do you have set aside so far?"

"I don't have any," said Hank Harrison. "You know that."

"How many delegates to the National Convention are pledged to you, right now, today?" asked the Party Chairman.

"None, of course," said Hank. "And you know that, too."

"Well," said the Party Chairman, "someone who has been on *Jeopardy!* ought to be able to figure out how many times someone has been nominated for President when just a few weeks before the National Convention he didn't have a nickel in his campaign fund and not even a single delegate backing him. Try, 'What is never?' "

# Thirty-three

President Hank Harrison was sitting at his desk reading some papers marked "Top Secret" when Kay Bolton opened the door to the Oval Office and informed him that the visitor that he had summoned had arrived. "Bring him right in," he said. As his guest entered the Oval Office, Hank stood up and walked over to greet him. "You probably know why I asked you to stop by for a private chat," he said.

"No, I really don't," said Bill Schulz.

"Well, sit down and make yourself comfortable and I'll give you some hints," said Hank Harrison. He motioned Schulz to sit down on one of the two white sofas near the fireplace. Then he sat on the one across from him. "It has nothing whatsoever to do with the United States Information Agency," he said.

"You're starting to remind me of Jack Newell," said Schulz.

"I take that as a high compliment," said President Harrison. "You see, I am an admirer of the late President. He was a man with convictions and he had the courage of his convictions. He loved his country and he served it well. He was a true patriot."

"I know that," said Bill Schulz. "I miss him."

"Kay tells me that you two were very close," said President Harrison. "In fact, she tells me that President Newell considered you to be his best friend."

"I am honored that he felt that way," said Bill Schulz. "I considered him my best friend—and also the finest man I have ever known."

"She tells me that he trusted you totally," said President Harrison. "That he had complete confidence in your political judgement. That he felt you always had his best interests at heart. She also tells me that he loved your sense of humor and enjoyed your company immensely."

"That's nice to hear," said Bill Schulz.

"Kay tells me you are the one I need," said Hank Harrison.

"Pardon?" said Bill Schulz.

"Every President needs someone he can depend on to level with him," said Hank Harrison. "A good friend who knows the score and who will help him keep things in proper perspective. Now I've got lots of good friends back in Freka, Arkansas, but I'm afraid none of them has any great interest in politics or government. Aren't a whole lot of people who stop by the dry-cleaners with ideas about political strategy, you know. So, upon Kay's recommendation, you are hereby drafted for the role. I have quickly come to have a lot of confidence in her. She makes being President a whole lot easier than it might otherwise be. Now, Bill, what do you say?"

"Are you sure?" said Bill Schulz. "You really don't know me."

"I like what I've seen and heard," said President Harrison. "If you were good enough for President Newell in that kind of role, I am sure you will be fine for me, too. I want us to have the same kind of arrangement."

"Mr. President . . ."

"Hank," said Hank Harrison, "I know that you called President Newell 'Jack' and I want you to call me 'Hank.' In private, of course, not in public."

"You seem to know a good bit about the relationship between Jack Newell and I, but . . ."

"Kay is a very good briefer," said Hank Harrison.

"Yeah, she's great," said Bill Schulz, "but I'm afraid there are things that even Kay doesn't know."

"You mean about Jack Newell's commitment to dump Bates and replace him with you?" asked Hank Harrison.

Bill Schulz was stunned. "Where did you get that idea?" he asked.

"I just told you," said President Harrison. "Kay is a remarkable briefer. You really are surprised that Jack Newell told her about it, aren't you? Bill, he told her because he felt that if anything ever happened to him—and he was a sick man, it turns out—well, he wanted people to know just how very highly he regarded you. He instructed her to someday reveal all this publicly whenever she felt the timing was appropriate. He thought it would be a nice tribute to you."

"I don't know what to say," said Schulz.

"Let me tell you some things about me," said Hank Harrison. And for the next hour and fifteen minutes Hank told Bill Schulz his life story, his philosophy of life and his thoughts on the major issues facing the nation and the world.

"So that's what you meant the other day about the Adams family," said Schulz. "Hey, don't go saying that to too many people. They'll think you're a bit . . ."

"Loony?" said Hank Harrison.

"It's an interesting footnote to history, your being related to the other two Harrison presidents," said Schulz.

Hank Harrison looked him square in the eye and said: "Bill, the other two Harrison presidents were footnotes in history. I intend to be more than that. I intend to seize the opportunity. Now, I told you what those clowns who came by had to say. My view is that someone sitting here in the White House as President and working closely with a skilled public relations guru who really knows political strategy and image-making, well, my view is that he has a hell of a good fighting chance. That's what I figure. Now tell me. Who's right—them or me?"

"I suppose you've got a chance," said Bill Schulz.

"Would you resign if you were me?" asked President Harrison.

"Hell, no," said Schulz.

"If you woke up tomorrow morning and found yourself President of the United States," asked Hank Harrison, "would you make a run for the Party nomination?"

"Hell, yes," said Schulz.

"Then what do you say?" asked President Harrison. "I would like to honor President Newell's commitment to you. How does a Harrison-Schulz ticket grab you?"

"I'll be damned," said Bill Schulz. "I'll be damned. And I'd say your odds just increased substantially." He made that remark lightly and with a big grin on his face. The two men both laughed.

For the next hour Hank Harrison and Bill Schulz talked political strategy. Schulz impressed upon Hank that "bold and perhaps highly unorthodox" steps were going to be required.

"We have got to make the American people try to put themselves in your shoes and identify with you," said Schulz.

Schulz urged that Hank do another television address to the nation. He said the one that Hank had done immediately after assuming the presidency had been fine, that it had helped reassure the country and put people a little more at ease, but what was needed now was "a truly bold stroke, something completely different."

He said he knew exactly the kind of speech that Hank should give to make the American people identify with him and start rooting for him. He started to explain his idea.

"Golly, golly," Hank kept saying. And then he would laugh.

Hank Harrison's eyes opened wider and wider as Bill Schulz outlined the speech that he had in mind. Schulz characterized it as "bold, unorthodox, somewhat offbeat."

" 'Somewhat offbeat?' " said Hank as he broke into loud laughter. "It's incredible! It sure would be different from any speech any of my predecessors ever delivered, wouldn't it?"

"Well, the situation is quite different, isn't it?" replied Schulz.

Bill Schulz remembered back to that day in New Hampshire when he had convinced then-Governor Newell to run for President. He could hear Jack Newell saying, "Who gives a shit? Why not?" He hoped Hank Harrison would say the same thing.

Hank Harrison did not say, "Who gives a shit? Why not?" He only said, "Why not?"

# Thirty-four

For years to come, public opinion polls would depict that almost nine out of ten Americans considered Hank Harrison's very unconventional speech the most memorable Presidential address to the nation that they had ever witnessed.

It opened the way they all do. Gabby television network news "anchors" killed time by repeatedly telling viewers that the President would be speaking shortly and by asking two or three of their network colleagues to take turns speculating on what the President was going to say, it being their view, apparently, that the viewing public couldn't speculate for themselves without such coaching or, heaven forbid, simply wait a few minutes and let the President just tell them himself what he had to say.

Suddenly the television screen showed a shot of the White House lighted up at night. Next came a dissolve to the Oval Office. There was President Hank Harrison sitting at the Presidential desk looking into the camera. He has a somber expression on his face. The American flag was on one side of him, the Presidential flag on the other. Photos of his wife and children were visible on the credenza behind him.

The only thing that looked different from the sort of presidential address to the nation to which the American people are so accustomed was Hank himself. It was the way Hank was dressed. That was different. Very different. Of course it was how he had dressed during his previous brief address. And it was how he had dressed while serving as "Honorary President" and before that as the winning contestant on *Presidential Jeopardy!* It was the way he always dressed back in Freka, Arkansas. It took some getting used to. Especially in a President of the United States.

He was wearing a plaid shirt. He had on a striped tie that clashed against the shirt. And he was wearing a checkered sports coat that clashed against both the shirt and the tie. His coat was unbuttoned and it was clear that he was also wearing suspenders, which happened to clash with the shirt and the tie and the coat, too.

"You're lucky I can talk him out of wearing that damned straw hat of his," Mattie-Faye had told the White House public relations officers who had appealed to her to get Hank to dress "a bit more conservatively." Hank had finally told them in no uncertain terms to back off because he was "not about to start putting on airs." Bill Schulz, of course, knew all along exactly what Hank would be wearing. He had advised Hank to "dress just like you normally would" and not to let anyone else try to dress him up. Schulz had done that intentionally.

Hank began his television address to the nation by noting that this was the second time in less than a week that he had asked for television time to speak to the American people. He said that when he gave the first address he had not expected to make another one for some time. He said something unexpected had come up and he wanted to discuss it with the American people.

"Yesterday," he said, "almost immediately upon my return to the White House following the funeral for President John Newell, a group of politicians came by to see me here in this office. They came to deliver an ultimatum to me. They told me, in effect, to get out of town and turn things over to them.

"They said that they didn't care what our Supreme Court said. They want me out of here. They didn't seem to care what's the law of the land. They even made fun of the fact that I did well on *Presidential Jeopardy!*

"Well, to tell you the truth, I'm as surprised as you are that I am sitting here in the Oval Office as your President. I didn't seek the office. You know that. But here I am. Some say it's just an accident. Some say it's destiny. Some say it's God's will. You decide.

"Now the question is: Should I listen to those politicians and throw in the towel, call it quits, and let them have their way?

"I want to talk with you, the American people, and let you in on how I look at it. I want to ask you to try to put yourself in my shoes and then tell me what you think I should do.

"That's why I have asked to speak with you this evening. I need your advice. I need to ask you: What do you think is right? What do you think is fair? What would you do if you were me? I guess I'm repeating myself a bit, but this is important.

"I'm not going to make any pretenses: I like being President. It's a great honor. I love this country and I have principles and ideas that I believe in and that I think would benefit America. The truth is, I'd prefer to stay. So now you know where I'm coming from. You decide for yourself how you'd feel if it were you.

"The case I'd make, of course, is that I am President because the Supreme Court of the United States ruled that I should be President. I know it surprised a lot of people. It sure surprised me. But you can't go any higher than the Supreme Court, can you? I guess that's why they call it 'Supreme.' So it seems right and fair, doesn't it?

"Now I know that people like to talk about the burden of the Presidency, and I know that there are some people out there—some of them in the news media, some of them in Congress, and, yes, some of them even right here in the Executive Branch that is supposed to be working for me—who are saying that I might not to up to the burden.

"Know what I say to all that burden business? Baloney! That's what I say.

"Just take a good look at this house, folks. You television people, please show the folks watching this program a nice view of this house, would you?" On millions of television screens across America came a shot of the front of the White House lighted up at night.

"Show them the back, too, would you, please," said Hank. And onto the screens came a nice view of the back of the White House lighted up at night.

"Now move the cameras in closer here, would you, please," he called out to the network television crews. Then from his desk he pulled out a large photo book of the White House. "Just take a look at this place, folks," he said.

He opened the big photo book and motioned for the television cameras to move in still closer. "This photo you are looking at is of the Yellow Oval Room. Not the Oval Office. That's where I am right now. No, this is the Yellow Oval Room. Nice, huh? Well, this is a room that the President and his family use as what they call a drawing room. You and I would call it a family room. Pretty neat family room, isn't it? See those draperies? They're real silk. And that carpet? Take a look at that carpet. It's what they call antique Turkish Hereke. Mattie-Faye and I had never before seen a carpet so stunningly beautiful.

"Just a second." Hank thumbed through the book. "Oh, here. Look at this." The camera zoomed in. "This is what they call the Center Hall. It's up in what they call the Family Quarters. You don't see many houses that have rooms as big as this hall, do you? Just look at that exquisite furniture. This is a sitting room for the President and his family. Nice, huh?"

Hank sat the book down on his desk and pulled out a stack of photographs from one of his desk drawers. "These photo books, even the best ones, never seem to show much of the Presidential bedroom," he said. "So I had the White House photographers get me some nice shots to show you."

Once again he motioned the television cameramen to zoom in close. "Isn't it nice? Mattie-Faye and I like it a lot. We never dreamed we'd have a bedroom like this.

"Oh, here's the bathroom. I don't know about you, but we don't have a bathroom right off our bedroom in our little house back in Freka, Arkansas."

He sat the photos aside and once again picked up the photo book. "Just a second," he said, as he thumbed through it again.

"Oh, here, look at this. This is called the State Dining Room. Pretty fancy, isn't it? It's where you entertain people for dinner if you're President. Just look at that magnificent silverware and crystal."

He turned the pages. "This is the Family Dining Room. Get a load of that chandelier. Bet that cost a bundle. If you think that's neat, take a look at this. This is called the President's Dining Room. Beautiful, isn't it? With all these nifty places to sit down and eat, it must be hard to be President and not gain a lot of weight."

He showed the Lincoln Bedroom and the Lincoln Sitting Room and remarked how much he and Mattie-Faye had enjoyed staying there while he was serving as "Honorary President." Then he showed the Queen's Bedroom and the Blue Room and the Green Room and the Map Room and the China Room and the Diplomatic Reception Room and the Treaty Room and the Cabinet Room and a couple of the entrances and corridors.

"This is probably my favorite room," he said, as he showed the Library. "I like to read a lot, you know. My mother always told me, 'Show me a reader and I'll show you a leader.' Well, I just love that room.

"Oh, here's the East Room. Huge, isn't it? It's where the President holds all those really big receptions and parties. You know, the ones you always see on television. The ones the celebrities like to go to."

Hank closed the photo book. "Pretty nice place, isn't it?" he said as he set the big book aside on his desk.

Then he looked straight into the television cameras. "Folks, take a guess how much it cost me and Mattie-Faye to live here. Go ahead. Take a guess." He paused.

"Nothing. Not a cent. Neat, huh?" He smiled.

"Now look out in the driveway." The television cameramen panned the driveway but they were uncertain what they were looking for. "See that car?" said Hank. "The big long black limousine." Onto the television screens came a shot of the Presidential limousine lighted up at night. "I get to ride in it whenever and wherever I want. It's got a television set in it, too. Can you believe that? A television set! It also has a refrigerator. A television set and a refrigerator right in the car. Incredible, isn't it?

"Suppose I want to go on a nice trip, maybe visit Fiji or Tonga or Rome or some other great spot in the world. Guess what? All I have to do is say I want to do it. That's all. No joke. Then when it's time to go all I have to do is walk out the back door and—guess what?—there's a helicopter waiting to take me to the airport. Right in my own back yard—a helicopter. Big one. And waiting for me at the airport is my own airplane. Not one of those little things. A great big stretched out 747. Neat, huh? It's got a bedroom and a shower. Queen sized bed, too. It folds out. It's a nice comfortable sofa during the daytime. Imagine that. Your own private sofa and queen-sized bed right there on your own jumbo jet airplane. What a way to fly! That airplane—it's the one they call *Air Force One*, you know—well, that airplane has all sorts of nifty things—telephones, television sets, fax machines, all sorts of high-tech gizmos. You name it—it's got it. Oh, and here's the really good part: I don't have to bother with check-in counters or any of that stuff. I don't even need a ticket!"

He was smiling a lot. And he sounded happy.

"Now suppose you are President and you and your wife want to have some interesting company over for dinner or something," he continued. "All you have to do is just ask the staff to make a few calls and next thing you know the Queen of England and her husband drop by for dinner. And—guess what?—Mattie-Faye doesn't have to do any of the cooking or serving. Nothing. She can just sit at the table like one of the guests and be waited on. Neat, huh?

"One of the really nifty things about living in the White House is that it comes with all sorts of servants who wait on you hand and foot. Get this—they even shine your shoes and set your clothes out for you in the morning. And when you want to take a bath one of the servants turns the water on for you. Can you believe that! I usually take a shower myself, but if someone else is turning on the water and keeping an eye on it, well, I just might take baths instead of showers a lot more often.

"Oh, about the Queen, they tell me that when she comes, she always invites you and your spouse to come stay with her and the Prince at their Palace and go riding horses with them. Sounds like a lot of fun to me. Have you ever stayed in a Palace? I haven't. Not yet.

"Or suppose you want to go to a concert. You know, maybe a Michael Jackson concert. Guess what? Michael will come right into your house and sing just about any song you request. Dance, too. Isn't that great? And you can bring a whole bunch of your friends. It's free. Doesn't cost you a cent.

"And get this. While you are having all this fun and doing all these interesting things—guess what?—they pay you two hundred thousand dollars a year to do it. Plus they give you a big expense account. Isn't that great?"

It was that kind of a speech.

At the end, Hank Harrison looked into the television cameras and said: "My friends, I haven't had the chance to do hardly any of these nifty things just yet. Hardly any of them. I've been kinda busy just settling in. But I'd sure like to do them. And Mattie-Faye would, too. So would the kids."

He paused briefly and then he fixed his gaze directly into the camera straight in front of him and said to the American people: "Now tell me the truth: if you had this, would you give it up?"

# Thirty-five

"Honest"—that's the word that was most often used to describe Hank Harrison's address to the nation.

"President Harrison was unpretentious and straightforward in his unusual address to the nation this evening," said Ted Koppel in introducing *Nightline's* report, "and early indications are that his refreshing sincerity and humility seem to have impressed an awful lot of people."

Four times on *Nightline* that evening Ted Koppel used the word "refreshing" when speaking about Hank's performance. Six times he used the word "honest." Each of the three guests *Nightline* picked to help analyze the speech used the word "honest" three or four times. And all three also agreed with *Nightline's* host that the speech was "refreshing."

"Hank Harrison may be inexperienced," said Dan Rather, leading off *CBS News'* evening report the following day, "but it looks like he's scoring points by being genuine." Rather's introduction was followed by a series of grass-roots interviews with typical citizens from different parts of the country. Every one of them used the word "honest" when describing their impressions of Hank's televised remarks. And every one of them used the word "refreshing."

On *ABC News* and *NBC News* and CNN, it was the same thing. Plenty of so-called typical citizens using words such as "honest" and "refreshing" and "genuine" and "sincere" and "humble" to describe the new man in the White House.

"If Richard Nixon had given a speech like that, instead of spouting all those pious platitudes claiming that the reason he didn't want to resign was because he was just trying to protect the institution of the Presidency, he probably would have weathered Watergate," observed the *Evans-Novak Report.*

Other columnists and newspaper editorial writers and radio and television commentators made the same or similar statements.

A Gordon S. Black Inc. public opinion poll showed that by an overwhelming margin the American people viewed the new President as "someone whose word you can believe." Every other major poll that followed showed the same thing.

The polls also showed that, again by a very wide margin, the American people agreed with the statement that this new President of the United States was "a person of common sense."

According to the polls, nine out of ten Americans were saying, hell, yes, if they had it, they'd keep it.

There was one reaction to the speech that even Bill Schulz had not anticipated: The White House was flooded with requests for tickets to the Michael Jackson concert.

# Thirty-six

The hard liners in control at the Kremlin felt that any new President should be tested. Just like the way it used to be back in the era that was now being referred to as "The First Cold War." Following a plan agreed to at a strategy session of the People's Council, the Russian Dictator placed a telephone call to the White House for his first conversation with President Hank Harrison.

Speaking through an interpreter, he began the conversation with an obvious lie. He said that he regretted that he had not been able to personally attend the funeral of President Newell.

President Harrison had his own interpreter at his side and spoke through him. "Your absence was noticed," he replied.

The Russian Dictator said that he hoped that he and the new President could develop a good working relationship in the interest of their two countries and "in the interest of world peace."

"That would be nice," said Hank. "It is also quite necessary, isn't it?"

Then came the punch. The Russian Dictator said that he and "the other leaders of the Union of Sovereign States" had some "deep concerns" about "certain impediments" that "not only make peace-making difficult, but indeed could make the situation quite precarious."

"Don't talk in puzzles," said Hank. "What are you trying to say?"

"Mr. President," said the Russian Dictator, "The Union of Sovereign States can no longer accept the massive U.S. naval deployment in the Persian Gulf area. We most certainly cannot any longer tolerate American war ships being based in Latvia, Estonia and Lithuania. Those are lands whose people wish to be allied with us, not with you."

"That's a crock," said Hank.

There was a pause on the line. The Russian Dictator cleared his throat and so did his interpreter. Then he continued talking: "And certainly you understand why we must demand the immediate withdrawal of all U.S. military advisors assisting the Government of Ukraine."

"Forget it," said Hank.

There was another pause on the line. Once again the Russian Dictator and his interpreter cleared their throats. Then he continued speaking: "We would hope that as a gesture of friendship and cooperation, and as a demonstration of your good faith, you will immediately make it clear that it is the intention of your Administration to take the appropriate steps to pull back from this dangerously threatening posture."

"Threatening to whom?" asked Hank.

"To the Union of Sovereign States," said the Russian Dictator. "To world peace. Certainly you recognize that. Certainly you see the need to act quickly to demonstrate that you are prepared to join with the Union of Sovereign States in renouncing imperialism and in making a firm commitment to the cause of peace."

"Are you trying to intimidate me?" asked Hank.

"Mr. President," said the Russian Dictator, "All that the Union of Sovereign States is asking is that you join us in the effort for greater peace and understanding. But I must impress upon you that we shall not back down from our efforts to promote peace and oppose imperialism. We are expecting you to take prompt action to insure that this tension is dealt with in a satisfactory manner. The consequences of failure to act could be most serious."

"The Chairman is very angry," said the Russian interpreter. "To properly translate, I must tell you his tone of voice is very important. He is most upset."

"It sounds put on," the President's interpreter whispered. "My bet is that it's a phony act and this line about his being angry and upset was scripted for his interpreter ahead of time."

"Look, fella," said Hank Harrison, "I'm busy. I've got important things to do. I know you guys probably think I'm just some hick you can push around, and maybe you feel you've got to find out, but forget it. I don't have time to play some silly game pretending there's an international crisis when there really isn't any crisis."

"Mr. President," interrupted the Russian Dictator, "I am most serious. The situation is most serious. To treat this crisis lightly would be a most dangerous miscalculation that could have the most serious consequences."

"Cut the crap," said Hank Harrison. "There's no crisis in the Persian Gulf. And there's no crisis in Latvia, Estonia or Lithuania. Or Ukraine, either. You know that. I know that. Anyone who knows anything knows that."

"You cannot ignore a crisis," shouted the Russian Dictator. In English. He said it in English.

"Hey, I didn't know you speak English," said Hank. "Hell, the CIA didn't know that. Wait till I tell them this one. I'll be damned. You didn't need that interpreter, did you? You were faking it. You're a sneaky son-of-a-gun, aren't you?"

"Some might say I'm a sneaky son-of-a-bitch," said The Russian dictator in perfect English, "but the important point right now is that we must deal with this important crisis."

"You guys want to play crisis, fine, go right ahead," said Hank. "But you are going to have to do it by yourselves. Understand that?"

"What are you saying?" asked the Russian Dictator. "I not understand."

"What I am saying," said Hank, "is that I don't give a damn what you say or do, but bear in mind that if you go and do anything that pisses me off, you are going to be sorry. Very sorry. I've got enough real problems right here, fella. I don't have to import any phony ones. Got that?"

"But, but, but, Mr. President," sputtered the Russian Dictator, "certainly you not want to start up the Cold War again, do you?"

"You're the ones who have been doing that," said Hank Harrison. "It was a nice recess we had going for awhile. We had a few good years. Too few. Damned shame. You and your murdering little gang destroyed a wonderful new beginning."

"Listen to me," said the Russian Dictator.

"No, you listen to me," said Hank. "Don't try a silly stunt like this ever again. Understand that?"

"You are threatening me," said the Russian Dictator. "I not understand. Why you threatening me?"

"No, you were trying to threaten me," said Hank.

"Is that all you have to say?" asked the Russian Dictator.

"No," answered Hank, "I have something else to say."

"Please go ahead," said the Russian Dictator.

"If you try any monkey business, fella, I am going to respond. Understand that? You say or do anything—anything!—that annoys me and the first thing I am going to do is invoke my Presidential authority to order McDonald's to immediately close down their Moscow restaurant."

"What the hell!" said the Russian Dictator.

"How would like to have everyone in Moscow holding you personally responsible for the fact that there is no longer a decent place to go out for dinner?" asked Hank.

On that note, Hank Harrison, President of the United States of America and leader of the Free World, said goodbye to the Russian Dictator and hung up the phone.

# Thirty-seven

When Bill Schulz learned from Hank Harrison about the Russian Dictator's attempt to intimidate the new President, he knew exactly what to do. He waited a couple of days to be sure it was indeed a bluff. Then he leaked it to some friends in the news media.

"RUSSIANS THROW A CRISIS, BUT NOBODY COMES," read the now classic banner headline in *The New York Post*.

"The Crisis That Never Was," *Nightline* billed its program about the Russian Dictator's attempted intimidation of the new President and what Ted Koppel referred to as President Hank Harrison's "cool and obviously very effective" response.

At the United Nations, the Russian ambassador accused the United States of reneging on its pledge to honor the UN pact against "the use of food as a political weapon."

The usual caravan of crazies poured into Lafayette Park across from the White House dressed up as if they were auditioning for roles as extras in a horror movie and carrying their usual all-purpose fill-in-the-blanks anti-USA signs.

On Capitol Hill, more than a few Members of Congress rushed to the microphones and television cameras to denounce the position of the President of the United States and express "understanding" of the Russian position, thereby assuring themselves a prominent place on the evening news.

On the New York Stock Exchange, McDonald's stock fell two points.

In Moscow, demonstrators took to the streets. The Russian news agency TASS estimated the crowd at 2,000. Western journalists on the scene reported that the mass demonstration drew closer to 250,000. The Russian citizens who poured into the streets created the biggest commotion Moscow had seen since the days of the historic August 1991 botched coup attempt.

To the amazement of the world, the signs the Russian demonstrators were carrying denounced the Russian Dictator and his cohorts for risking the closing of the Moscow McDonald's.

Inside the Kremlin, the Russian Dictator met with the members of the People's Council to discuss strategy. They knew it would be a long meeting, so they sent out for lunch from their favorite restaurant—McDonald's.

"The American President is right," said the Minister for Agriculture. "If he orders it closed, there won't be a decent place left to eat in Moscow."

"We think we know what the CIA stooge Harrison is up to," said the Chief of Intelligence.

"Ah, shut up," said the Russian Dictator. "A few days ago you were telling us that the Americans were going to invade the Middle East. You were telling us that Newell wasn't dead."

"I said we thought he might be alive," said the Chief of Intelligence. "We felt the odds were 50/50."

"You dumb shit!" said the head of the Red Army. "There is a 100% chance that anyone is either dead or alive. So there's a 50/50 chance whichever way you guess. What the hell do you people do for intelligence gathering, flip coins?"

"Hey," said The Minister For Defense, "I order Big Mac. This is Quarter Pounder."

"The point is," said the Russian Dictator, "this damned dry-cleaner has called our bluff."

"What are we going to do?" asked the Minister for Oil and Gas.

"That's what we are here to decide," said the Russian Dictator.

They discussed all sorts of options. Some advocated naval maneuvers in the Persian Gulf. The argument against that was that by the time enough Russian ships arrived in the area to create any sort of an effective crisis atmosphere too much time would have passed and the news media's short attention span would have long since turned the focus to other matters.

Some proposed air maneuvers close to the South Korean border. The argument against that was that if they rushed into it and made the mistake of sending pilots who had not been sufficiently screened there was a considerable risk of defections and that would be severely embarrassing.

"You mentioned Europe in your threat," the Minister for Coal said to the Russian Dictator. "Why don't we have the Warsaw Pact make some threatening moves?"

"You dimwit!" said the head of the Red Army. "There is no Warsaw Pact anymore. It's gone. That imbecile Gorbachev gave it all away. All he cared about was impressing a few people in the West and conning them into giving him the Nobel Peace Prize. What a disgrace to the memory of Lenin and Stalin!"

"Yeltsin was even worse," said the Minister for Transportation. "Thank God we got rid of those two fools."

"Thank who?" said the Russian Dictator.

"It's just an expression," apologized the Minister for Transportation.

The Russian Dictator and his so-called People's Council spent three hours in the Kremlin reviewing American and allied performance in the world in recent years and arguing about possible American responses to any moves that they might make. Then they made their decision.

The show of hands depicted a close margin for the course of action that the Russian Dictator clearly favored. Much as the Kremlin gang opposed the idea of letting others vote on anything of importance, they themselves liked to put things to a vote within the group. A vote that only they witnessed, of course.

The Russian Dictator issued the statement they agreed upon. As always, he lied and said that it was a unanimous decision. The statement asserted that "as a gesture of friendship" to "our new friend in the White House," the Union of Sovereign States wished to "correct this unfortunate misunderstanding" and "assure the new President and the American people of our good will and spirit of cooperation in the interest of better relations and for the cause of world peace and understanding."

The statement included an announcement from the Russian Dictator that he was proposing a new educational exchange program. The statement also contained another interesting announcement: The Union of Sovereign States was ending Russian support to their puppet, the dictator of Cuba, support which he and his associates had reinstated following their successful coup. He was, of course, lying about this, too.

Within a half hour following the release of the Russian statement, the U.S. Ambassador in Moscow entered the office of the Russian Dictator and delivered to the Kremlin the promised secret message from the President of the United States. It contained a pledge not to close the Moscow McDonald's.

Hank Harrison was compared to Truman during the Berlin crisis, Kennedy during the Cuban Missile Crisis, Reagan at Grenada and Bush at Panama and Kuwait.

McDonald's stock recovered its two point drop and added seven eighths of a point.

All the major public opinion polls showed that the American public's concern about Hank Harrison's inexperience was easing off significantly.

The polls also showed that his "leadership" ratings were sharply on the rise.

That was the good news.

The bad news for Hank Harrison was that he didn't have any money to run a campaign for the nomination. He had checked out the Party Chairman's figures. And the best estimate he could make was that he would indeed need at least $125 million. Real quick.

# Thirty-eight

After clearing the idea with President Hank Harrison, Bill Schulz called the Party Chairman and suggested that the two of them meet and talk things over.

"There's a Cabinet post in it for you if you bring Harrison around and get him to give the nomination speech for Bernie," the Party Chairman told Schulz.

"A Cabinet post? Is that so?" said Schulz.

"Bernie thinks he could fit you in as Secretary of Commerce," said the Party Chairman.

"Perhaps you might want to inform 'The Jerk' that Vice Presidents do not pick the Cabinet," said Schulz.

"That's not a very smart thing for you to say, Schulz, ole boy," said the Party Chairman. "I'm going to pretend I didn't hear that. Then I won't have to tell Bernie. But from here on in, I think you'd be wise to bear in mind that Bernie's not going to be Vice President much longer."

"Exactly," said Schulz. "Come January 20th, he's going to be the former Vice President."

"You think Stupp can beat him?" asked the Party Chairman. "Just because of that scene at Andrews? Hell, that'll blow over. That's why he's been keeping such a low profile right now. Bernie's handling it correctly now. He's listening to me. Letting things just sit. Not challenging in the courts or making strong statements. Playing along with this Supreme Court plot for now and getting ready to settle scores later. Just get the nomination and then turn the focus on Stupp and drive up his negatives. They'll probably both have very high negatives by the time Election Day rolls around. I figure that will turn voters off and drop the turnout a good bit and I figure that will help us."

"The President is running," said Bill Schulz. "You can get on the bandwagon now or you can just stand there and get run over by it. Take your pick. That's what I'm here to tell you. The President is giving you one hour to re-think things and then make your stand. You can come with us or you can go to hell."

" 'The President,'" said the Party Chairman in his most sarcastic tone. "Don't make me laugh! You mean 'The Dry-cleaner.'"

"Shall I report to the President that you have decided to pass on the opportunity to be on the team and continue to have an important role to play?" asked Schulz.

"I have an important role to play," shot back the Party Chairman, "and I'm going to play it. I'm going to head up the campaign for Bernie Bates. And Bernie is going to be nominated. And Bernie is going to be elected President. And I am going to go into the Cabinet. And you are not."

The Party Chairman said that under no circumstances would he step aside and permit Hank Harrison to select a successor. He reminded Bill Schulz that his term didn't expire for a few months. He acknowledged that normally a Party Chairman would step aside if that was the wish of the President but said he considered Bernie Bates as rightfully President and Bates wanted him to stay put.

"It takes money to get nominated for President," said the Party Chairman. "It takes millions, and Hank Harrison doesn't have squat."

"You think money's everything, huh?" asked Schulz.

"What's everything," said the Party Chairman, "is being on television all the time. Not the evening news. Not those public affairs shows. Not even those television addresses to the nation, although I must admit the one he just did was damned clever. No, Schulz, ole boy, it's not the money, it's what the money buys. You've got to be on television all the time, but you've got to be in those nice slick 30 second messages that Joe and Jane Six-Pack can't escape from. Those expensive spots that run over and over and over. You've got to be able to intrude while people are watching their dopey shows. That's what you need all that money for. Certainly you understand that, don't you? Hell, of all people, you should understand that."

"Thank you," said Schulz.

"For what?" asked the Party Chairman.

"You'll see," said Schulz.

# Thirty-nine

The Sunday night movie on ABC had been heavily promoted and it was drawing a huge audience despite the fact that it was in black-and-white. It was one of America's greatest film classics—*Harvey.*

Ten minutes into the movie the screen turned black. Then a strong deep voice was heard.

"Ladies and Gentlemen," the announcer said in a most dramatic fashion, "We interrupt this program to bring you a message from the President of the United States."

Onto the screen came a night view of the White House.

The camera zoomed in to a closer shot of the White House and then dissolved to a view of the Oval Office.

President Hank Harrison was sitting behind the Presidential desk. The American flag on one side of him. The Presidential flag on the other. Pictures of his wife and children visible on the credenza behind him. He had a somber expression on his face.

"My fellow Americans," began the President.

Across the nation, millions of Americans sat on the edge of their chairs, holding their breath, their eyes glued to the television screen.

"The situation in the Middle East," he continued.

"*Uh-oh*," millions of Americans thought to themselves.

". . . gives me the kind of headache that ordinary aspirin can't handle. That's why I use Excedrin."

"What the hell!" screamed Herb Stupp as he sat at home reviewing the draft of a campaign speech.

"Holy shit!" shouted the Party Chairman.

Vice President Bernie Bates looked down at the drink he was holding in his hand and said something foul. Then he threw his glass against his living room wall.

A few minutes later, on CBS, another program was interrupted by another dramatic sounding announcement: "We take you now to the White House for an important announcement."

And there was President Hank Harrison standing in the Presidential bathroom wearing nothing but a towel around his waist. The President of the United States turned toward the camera and held up a can of Arrid Extra Dry spray deodorant.

"You know," he said, "being President of the United States can sometimes have its tense moments. So I probably need to worry more than you do about perspiration. Because I'm in the public eye so much, I have to be extra concerned about feeling fresh and being dry. The way I look at it, if the President offends, the nation offends. So for your sake as well as my own, I use Arrid Extra Dry."

Viewers whose television dials were set to the NBC program saw Hank Harrison appearing in a commercial for Kellogg's Corn Flakes.

Same sort of dramatic introduction. Then a shot of Hank sitting at the breakfast table with Mattie-Faye. He poured corn flakes into a bowl and then picked up a pitcher of milk and poured some over the corn flakes.

He picked up the box of Kellogg's Corn Flakes, looked at it and smiled. Then he turned back and looked into the camera. "You know," he said, "when you're in politics you come across all sorts of flakes. In fact, Washington is famous for its flakes." He held up the box of Kellogg's Corn Flakes. "Here's the flakes I prefer," he said. "I've had it with all those other flakes I have to deal with."

On CNN Hank was appearing in an ad urging people to subscribe to *Time* magazine. "Son of a bitch!" screamed the editor of *Newsweek*. "I want to know what dopey reporter of ours got him upset with us."

Some columnists and commentators complained about the propriety of the President of the United States endorsing products. But the general public seemed to buy the White House's rebuttal.

This was really nothing new, claimed the Presidential Press Secretary. After all, the words and actions of Presidents have long influenced consumer purchasing decisions. Jelly-bean sales soared because Ronald Reagan made a point of the fact that he liked them. Broccoli sales fell when George Bush make a point of banning that vegetable from Presidential presence. And one hell of a lot more rocking chairs were sold in America after John F. Kennedy made such a point of sitting in one in the Oval Office.

The Presidential Press Secretary pointed out that every product Hank Harrison had endorsed was American-made. "If the President of the United States can't say a good word about fine American products, how do you think that would look to people who are comparing our products with those of our foreign competition?" he asked.

On television, on radio, in newspapers, in magazines and on billboards, overnight Hank Harrison became America's most popular pitchman, pushing some of America's most popular products.

The companies whose products he endorsed saw to it that campaign funds poured into the Hank Harrison For President Campaign Committee. And because people do not contribute to Presidential campaigns only out of gratitude but also out of fear or the desire to court favor, those companies that were competitors of the producers of the products he endorsed also suddenly opened their wallets and contributed heavily to the Hank Harrison For President Campaign Committee.

And then those companies selling products competing with products Hank had endorsed approached President Harrison through Bill Schulz and asked for equal time for their products. "Why not?" said Bill Schulz.

And so Hank Harrison appeared in advertisements for both Coke and Pepsi. For Bufferin and Tylenol as well as Excedrin. For six different brands of breakfast cereals. For GM cars and Ford cars and Chrysler cars.

No beer ads. No shots of him with a cigarette. No foreign products. Nothing that Bill Schulz thought might be in any way controversial. But just about anything else was fair game.

On Madison Avenue Hank Harrison became the candidate to back. He was great for business. Every major corporation in America was expanding its advertising budget. The advertising and public relations professionals never had it so good. Not surprisingly, lots of the best creative minds in the business showed their appreciation by lining up to volunteer their services to the Hank Harrison For President Campaign Committee.

Media owners were, of course, thrilled. Never before had there been such a sharp increase in advertising revenues.

Some columnists and commentators implied that after President Harrison began endorsing products and ad revenues increased so dramatically most of the news media began to put a noticeably more pro-Harrison slant into their reports. Not many people paid much attention to that charge. Not many cared.

America's business leaders were ecstatic—the public was suddenly in an incredible buying mood. Inventories were dropping sharply and corporate profits were increasing at record levels. Organized labor was elated, too—the increased demand for consumer goods was spurring the economy and creating new jobs by the thousands.

And the stock market was heading up, up and away.

Hank Harrison seemed to be just the sort of "regular guy" that the American people like and yearn for.

There was an ebullient spirit sweeping the land. The voters of America were in a very happy, almost festive, mood.

And delegates to the National Convention were very impressed.

# Forty

When the Party met at its convention in Denver, Colorado, Hank Harrison of Freka, Arkansas, the third Harrison President, was nominated for President of the United States on the first ballot. There was no opposition.

Every major public opinion poll showed him leading former television star Herb Stupp by at least a 23% margin. And if that held up, and all signs indicated that it would, Hank was headed for perhaps the greatest landslide victory in American history.

Word had gone out that he was going to dump Bernie Bates. Not very many people cared.

The dry-cleaner from Freka, Arkansas, gave a fine acceptance speech. It was interrupted fifty-five times with applause. The delegates who had gathered in Denver's *Skydome* had every reason to cheer and shout. They knew that they were going with a winner.

The morning following his nomination, Hank Harrison announced the name of his choice for Vice President. And that evening, by acclamation, William Schulz of Clifton, Virginia, became the person who was all but guaranteed to become, as the speakers giving the nominating and seconding speeches kept putting it, "the next Vice President of the United States."

The polls showed that less than five percent of the American public claimed to have ever heard of Bill Schulz prior to his being selected by President Hank Harrison. And just about every single one of those polled who claimed to have previously heard of Schulz was, of course, patently lying just to try to make himself appear more knowledgeable.

Some columnists and commentators questioned whether Schulz's background and experience were sufficient for the Vice Presidency.

But, of course, only a scant few people in the entire country really cared all that much about who was running for Vice President.

Bill Schulz cared.

Bernie Bates cared.

A few others cared.

Including now, of course, a number of the members of The American Association of Political Consultants who were kicking themselves silly because they had never thought to try what Bill Schulz had dared and done.